OVERCOMING
FEAR

The exciting story about one man's struggle
and triumphant victory over fear.

Walt Croom
with Elaine Huber

Overcoming Fear
Christian Counseling Publications

Copyright © 1999
Walter Allen Croom
PO Box 878
Aberdeen, Maryland 21001

1st printing, 1999

ISBN: 0-7392-0149-2

Printed in the USA by

MORRIS PUBLISHING
3212 East Highway 30 • Kearney, NE 68847 • 1-800-650-7888

Acknowledgements

Grateful acknowledgment is made to the following for permission to use copyright material:

Rodeheaver Company
>   Excerpt from *In the Garden* by
>   C. Austin Miles, © 1940 by Rodeheaver Co.

Hope Publishing Company
>   Excerpt from *Great is Thy Faithfulness* by
>   Thomas O. Chisholm, © 1951 by Hope
>   Publishing Co.

Lillenas Publishing Company
>   Excerpt from *He Giveth More Grace* by
>   Annie Johnson Flint, © 1941 by Lillenas
>   Publishing Co.

I offer public acknowledgment to Mrs. Elaine Huber for carefully editing this manuscript. Her help as a freelance writer proved invaluable. To Mrs. Huber I am deeply indebted.

I extend appreciations to the following for reading this manuscript and offering their thoughts: Dr. Daniel Peters; Mr. Gary Foster; Mrs. Evelyn Smith; Retired Chaplain (Col.) and Mrs. Jack C. Randles; Miss Joy Croom; and Mrs. Pat Didden. I thank Mrs. Adrienne Walker and Mrs. Trish Glover for spending many hours at the computer typing and retyping.

I also thank my dear wife Judy for her understanding and patience as I worked on this project.

To Mother

Table of Contents

1 In The Beginning...

I don't know if there's any truth to the old adage that you learn what you grow up with. Yet I knew fear so much of my life that I now wonder if I cuddled up with it early in life. If I did, I certainly didn't realize I was doing it.

The middle of the twentieth century—1948, to be exact—should have been an unthreatening time to be born. World War II was over. So was rationing. Harry Truman was president, and the Cleveland Indians had even beaten the Boston Red Sox in the World Series!

At the time I enlarged the Croom family to five, home was an unpainted wood house along a dirt lane near the small town of Richlands, North Carolina. There was no indoor plumbing and the walls were plastered with newspaper to keep the cool air out during the winter months.

Just up the road, on a small farm, lived my grand-dad. It must have been a good place to grow up because Dad had at least one good memory. I remember him often speaking about picking up Indian arrowheads each spring. They were especially easy to spot because the first plowing of the spring exposed them and the warm sun sparkled off their flint edges. In the corner of one of the fields could still be seen an old Indian burial ground. Maybe there lay the owners of those arrowheads. At any rate, Indians had once roamed those fields. Maybe they had been Tuscarora Indians, a powerful branch of Iroquois who before

1

1713 had wandered in from the coastal plains and befriended white settlers. But guns and liquor had brought slavery and crime, so the Tuscaroras had turned savage and then drifted slowly away to Pennsylvania and New York.

When the Crooms left their native England and settled in what is now Onslow County, North Carolina, I have yet to learn. It is clear that the surname Croom had been an early one in the East Riding of Yorkshire and in Worcestershire, England, and research has uncovered it as far back as the tenth century in William the Conqueror's Doomsday Book. But when kings had turned tyrants, life here promised better things. The Mortons, my mother's family, had also left Great Britain for the same reason, and so it was here—in a community where a fellow could hear lingering Elizabethan accents if he listened closely—that my grandfather had purchased farms in 1933 and 1934—and later my mother and father had met and I had been born.

A year or so after I arrived, Mom and Dad moved up the road to another old house which I think may have once been slave quarters. I have no conclusive proof of that, but I do know that old house had been built long before the Civil War. Set along a dirt lane lined by mature trees, it was much like the one in which I had been born. A pump sat on the front porch and in the back yard stood an outhouse. The porch, the outhouse, and the house itself were all made of weatherboard, probably chestnut or some other hardwood, unpainted like most of the other old tenant houses that dotted the landscape of the South. Most people couldn't afford such luxuries. Besides, painting his house every three or four years was a job a fellow overbusy in the fields just didn't need.

The farm on which we lived joined Granddad's farm. Granddad's farm stood next to Mr. Marshburn's farm where Dad had spent his boyhood days working. Dad had grown up on a farm, so it had been natural for him to work on somebody's farm. Everyday Dad walked the full length of his daddy's land, up past the Cavanaugh cemetery and on past the old Indian burial ground to where Mr. Marshburn's house stood on a small hill surrounded by large beautiful trees.

When I was growing up, Dad was a sharecropper for Mr. Marshburn, so I too had memories of farm life. Here my brothers and I got a good "licking" for cutting a hole in my mother's new red vinyl sofa. My brother Phil found Mr. Marshburn's 1951 green Plymouth irresistible and often grabbed hold of its bumper as it bounced down the lane by our little house. I can still see him bobbing up and down with hard bumps as he was dragged along. I pulled my own tricks too. I recall once hitting a chicken with a stick. The chicken fell over dead, so, trying to destroy the evidence, I picked it up and carried it to the old outhouse. Just as I was about to pitch it in, that "dead" chicken began flapping its wings and flew away. Was I ever relieved!

Most people who lived in our county were farmers. They either owned their own farm, or, like my dad, worked as tenant farmers until they were able to save enough money to purchase their own land. Though most of them grew cotton, corn, soybeans and peanuts, tobacco was king. Western areas of the state—cities like Winston-Salem, Charlotte, and the state capitol, Raleigh, were developing some industry thanks to good roads and a decent rail system. But the lowlands were less favored and not progressing as well. Long before, the Civil War had so obliterated the

South's economy that most people would never rival a Northern standard of living. Yet, because they had work, they could at least be sure of plenty to eat.

Financially, Dad was doing the best he had ever done. Some of that certainly came from harvesting tobacco, but I didn't realize that the rest of it came from the cases of liquor he stashed in the back of the car after he took out the back seat. I just knew that he covered those cases with a blanket so we kids had a place to sit when we went away in the car. Now I know he was selling it to a distributor who then resold it to nearby country folks.

Dad was a proud man, and though he didn't seem to be chasing a rainbow or the proverbial pot of gold at the end of it, his drinking did make him quickly wear out his welcome. So, rather than stay and meet problems head on, he—like the proverbial rolling stone that gathered no moss—just moved on to another farm.

The first move I remember was in 1954, when I was six. Again, things seemed calm enough. The New York Giants had won the World Series. Dwight D. Eisenhower, our hero from World War II, was now president, and the country would soon be rid of all Communist plots, thanks to Joe McCarthy's infamous anti-Communist hearings. And even though no "white folks" yet allowed "black folk" at their kitchen tables, stores and churches were populated by either "black" or "white." The Supreme Court had forced school desegregation with its Brown vs. Education decision. There were only several things that brought me apprehension—a big storm that blew in from the East Coast ...and the consequences of a little trick I pulled that literally blew up in both my brother's face and unleashed another episode of the anger Dad unpredictably vented on both me and the whole family.

One day my younger brother, Phil, childishly held up his hand and asked me to hit it. I had an air rifle in my hands, so I rather unthinkingly pulled it up to my shoulder and pulled the trigger. Of course, I missed his hand, but the shot hit him dead center between the eyes. A half inch in either direction, and he would have lost an eye. He screamed at the top of his voice as blood rushed down his face. Mother and LeAnna, an old black lady that worked as my mother's servant for room and board and a small stipend, rushed to my brother's aid. Dad scurried for a good firm stick. I got a thrashing I have never been able to erase from memory. After that, I quickly developed a survival mentality. I simply obeyed, the one and only thing that kept me out of reach of Dad's vengeance.

Though Mother usually compensated for Dad's sometimes cruel treatment of us kids by going to the other extreme, Dad refused to tolerate anything he deemed disobedience. The only grade he looked at on our report cards was the conduct grade. "Boy, you might not be able to learn," he would drawl, "but there's no excuse to disobey." Ironically, it was Dad who most disobeyed. He continued to make liquor and sell it. And, of course, he continued to drink. Once, when sheriffs came to the house to check out rumors that he was making and selling alcohol, Dad shoved his homemade brew beneath the covers of my older brother's bed, apparently not caring that Donald trembled in fear that he might end up looking down the barrel of a rifle. Dad eluded the law another time by setting fire to the evidence—his liquor still. Dad's new pickup truck also met the same fate when Dad decided not to continue payments. That same year when Dad hired some Alabama workers to harvest his crops, Houston, a young Creek Indian, came with them and, seeing the drunkenness and abuse of my father, reached out in kindness. What that offer of kindness did, however, was to make my fourteen-year-old sister disappear with him one week after my father had unmercifully lashed out at her. Houston had probably intended only friendship, but my sister read it as an offer of escape and took the easiest way out. When Charlotte returned home for a brief visit several years later, Dad went into her bedroom and destroyed all of her personal belongings. Of course, she never again visited while Dad remained at home with us.

Shortly after my sister left home, Dad gave up both farming and moonshining. For Mother, the move was a mixed blessing. He had stopped making the stuff, but he didn't stop drinking. It just got worse. With more drinking came more violence. I didn't really understand why my sister had left; I was only six. I just knew that something was terribly wrong. So I began to cling to my mother, often following her from room to room. I doubt if I could have put into words what I now know was wrong. I was afraid.

2 The Man I Knew

Dad didn't seem to notice my fear. He just rounded me up with the rest of the family and moved us all— again. This time we settled between Jacksonville and Richlands along the gum branch highway in an area nicknamed the "half moon," probably because it was a copy of a "half moon" street in long-ago native England. The only thing the area was noted for was that Edward Dudley, the first governor of North Carolina, had lived near by. Other than that piece of historical information, it was a dot in the road with just plain ordinary country folk who paid their taxes, raised their children, and lived in a neighborly way. The place was our home for the next five years.

The house we moved into was just another weathered board house, but it became the center of both very fond memories and unforgettable fears. The dilapidated old house had no running water, so the "rest room" was about fifty yards from the back door. Since we didn't have a bathtub, mother heated the water on the kitchen stove and we bathed with a wash cloth and towel. Using a garden hose, Dad constructed an outdoor shower that we used during the summer months.

This old unpainted house was literally built around a coal stove that sat in our living room. Around this central room were two bedrooms, a small kitchen, and, in time, even a bathroom. During the day, we kept the bedroom doors closed to conserve energy; then, during the night we left the bedroom doors stand open so heat could temper the bedrooms as we slept.

My brothers and I shared one of the two bedrooms. We slept on a genuine "feather" bed that we could literally mold around our little bodies. That could be pretty cozy on cold nights. And with a tin roof over our heads, we would sometimes fall asleep as loud raindrops tapped out a lullaby. During the school week, bedtime was at 9:00 p.m., but I often lay awake thinking for a while before I fell asleep. Sometimes those thoughts were less than sleep-inducing—like in 1959—when the Russians shot a rocket at the moon, only to have it miss its mark and speed on past. I was lying awake in bed and heard my dad comment, "If we ever hit the moon, we will all be destroyed." I cringed with fear under my blankets.

Something else quite dreadful lurked in the corners of my mind—the possibility of contracting the feared disease of the day—polio. Lying in bed, waiting for sleep, I often thought of how awful it would be to come down with it. Occasionally, I got up and stood by my bed to assure myself I could still walk. At school I couldn't ignore the nagging reality of Larry "Sunshine." He was a happy little fellow, but he had fallen victim to polio and had to walk with crutches even though he was in braces from the waist down. Sure, Jonas Salk's polio vaccine was on the market, but that did little to waylay my fear. I just never managed to run out of things to fear. Why, all around our school hung fallout shelter signs to remind me that the Kremlin and the White House were hardly friends.

Thankfully, I found some diversion in the company of Steve. He was the young son of a Marine who lived in the small mobile home park next to our tenant house. At the end of the park was a small pond where

Steve and I spent endless hours fishing. I found special delight in sitting on the bank of that pond with a friend my age, a pole in my hand, and a great big sky hovering over my head. In our blue jeans, flannel shirts, and tennis shoes, Steve and I sat there for hours at a time. Then, when we thought we had fished the pond empty, we would take off to the woods to look for a new fishing hole that held even greater promise.

Such comfortable times tempted me to suppose that life was less threatening than it actually was. True, Dad was no longer farming. Instead, he had—as he termed it—taken up "public work." Of course, since he was neither able to read nor write, his "work" became whatever employment he could find—mostly house painting. But that was a whole lot better than the bootlegging he had been doing earlier.

It wasn't that Dad appeared threatening. His five feet, ten inches were topped with dark hair, and under a high forehead were deep brown eyes that occasionally showed quickly extinguished sparks of warmth. And though the tobacco he chewed and the large cigars he smoked may have been a sort of pollution we could have done without, they, at the time, seemed harmless enough. Actually, he didn't seem all that bad—when he was sober.

Dad spent a part of his sober evenings watching the news on television. I'm sure he had not calculated any benefits beyond his own distraction or relaxation. He just cared what was occurring beyond his home. But since I wanted his approval, I too sat down and watched. Together, the two of us probably took in most every major event of the times.

As a six-year-old, I recall watching the McCarthy anti-Communist hearings. Later, it was the troops returning home from Korea. After President Kennedy's death, I happened to be watching when Jack Ruby pulled a gun and permanently silenced Lee Harvey Oswald. I never saw Dad become overly exercised by any of the things we watched. At least he never turned into an activist of any kind. He just voted, and would probably have made a valuable contribution to the society he moved in had he been privileged with proper guidance and training. I, too, found myself increasingly fascinated by what was occurring in the world, but I often wished I could go to bed sure that God had things under control.

Dad may not have had too good a track record living up to his own high standards, but he certainly attempted to reproduce them in us children. He tolerated no back talk. We were children, and we were to be more seen than heard. If ever we were allowed to be heard, there was no exchange of ideas. Expressing personal opinions was not something that was done in our home. The one thing that was enforced both inside and outside of our home were the social graces of the South. "Yes, Sir," "No, Sir," "Yes, Ma'am," "No, Ma'am" were the only ways we were allowed to address either Dad or Mom or any other adult.

But even if we obeyed out of fear, we did obey, and Mom often passed along compliments people in the community had given her concerning our good behavior. Dad made sure we walked the "straight and narrow."

Another thing Dad stressed was the importance of keeping a commitment. A man's handshake was supposed to be as good as a man's bond. Or as Dad proverbialized it, "Your word is your bond." At the time, I had no idea what he meant by that. What I did know was that what came out of Dad's mouth was dangerous. It was a constant stream of profanity. If I could have muted his foul language, he would have had virtually nothing left to say.

No way could such a habit have been blamed on Dad's lack of education—not even on the fact that his dad and mom had been just as educationally deprived. Rather, it was the result of his having grown up in a home where neither parent had been a Christian and no Christian values or principles had been taught.

Perhaps it was for the same reason that Dad had turned to strong drink. Frequently, on Friday nights after he had stopped by the local fish market and purchased the catch of the day, he would stroll over to the ABC store and buy a fifth of liquor.

The problem was that when Dad drank, he often became hostile. Much of that hostility he directed toward Mom. True, she at times was quite cynical and overly critical—a trait she had picked up from her own mother—but never was her cynicism any justification for the verbal and sometimes physical abuse that Dad sometimes inflicted on her.

Really, we all learned to keep our distance when Dad came home from work drunk. Unfortunately, he never was able to just "sleep it off." It seemed he had to work off his bingeing with some kind of cruelty. On two different occasions, when Dad had lost control of himself, Mom had to call the sheriff's department to the house and let them shoot tear gas into the house to calm things down. I realized that often our family was the talk of the community, and I wasn't exactly proud that during one round of Dad's misconduct, his picture hit the front page of the Jacksonville Daily News.

Alcohol had trapped Dad. Apparently, even he recognized that because sometimes as he sat in front of the television listening to some evangelist sharing the gospel, he wept uncontrollably. It was obvious that he hurt inside and it appeared that he really did not want to act out as he did. But no one in our family knew how to help, and few in the community showed any interest.

Mother understood that when Dad was under the influence of alcohol, he was capable of doing almost anything, so she did her best to keep us out of harm's way. Once, that meant leading us through the nearby swamp to higher ground and physical safety. Another time, she had to step between me and Dad because when Dad came home drunk and discovered I had accidentally broken my arm, he attempted to punish me, sure I had been "irresponsible" and needed correction. For me, it was confusing that one day my dad would punish me for something I couldn't avoid, and the next day—when he had sobered up—give me money to buy toys. It seemed he had two very distinct personalities.

Sober, Dad was a quite responsible, hard-working man. Like the earlier Puritans, he believed in the Biblical dictum that "If a man does not work, neither should he eat." Even when things were tough, he would not accept welfare. He believed that if a child was raised without learning to do something useful, that child would probably grow up to be "good for nothing." He saw to it that that wouldn't happen to me.

One summer I spent ten to twelve hours a day harvesting tobacco under a very hot sun. It was the hardest work I was ever to do. The farmer, however, urged us on with just the right kind of incentive.

"Boys, just make it to the end of the row and I will have a cool refreshing Pepsi Cola for you," he'd coax. Those rows seemed like an eternity long, but with the other fellows, I somehow managed to "hang in there" and make it to the end of each row and that good cold Pepsi Cola. I guess that's where I also got something else called endurance—the ability to keep on going when all the odds seemed against me.

At the end of that particular summer, Mom took my earnings and purchased my school clothing. She even managed to stretch it far enough to reward me with an inexpensive Zebco rod and reel for fishing. From that point on I purchased my own clothes, never once entertaining the notion that Dad and Mom may have been wrong to make me work so hard. Not only did I learn to reach for the "better," but I also internalized what had helped lots of boys before me grow up to make their mark on society—a good work ethic.

Dad was also always looking for smaller projects for me to do. Once, when he sent me to the forest to cut wood, I suggested, "Daddy, we don't burn wood." "I know," he said, "but you never know when we might need it." According to my dad, an idle mind was the devil's workshop. I guess—more than most—Dad knew that from experience.

As a painter, Dad found it necessary to work in other towns. On one occasion, Mother and I took a bus to Charleston, South Carolina to visit with him. That time he actually spent time with us. But before we left, he got drunk and picked a fight with his own brother who was also working in the same town.

This side of Dad's unpredictable personality caused lots of problems for the whole family. Sometimes, things got so out of hand at home that Mother packed our bags and moved us in with her mother until Dad had had enough time to "cool down." Once, when Mom had taken such an action, Dad decided to show his great displeasure, so he made my older brother and me spend the Christmas holidays away from home. We passed the first night on the back porch of my uncle's house. I still remember shivering and shaking and thinking my toes were going to freeze off. The next several nights it was lounging out with a few of my dad's whiskey-drinking buddies. Soon, a deputy sheriff was out hunting us. When the lady of the house answered the door, I heard the officer mention my mother's name. I wanted to run to the door, but I was too afraid to do anything but sit there and cry. My mother's name was the sweetest name I knew, and I had been separated from her. That lady tried keeping things peaceful by lying about our whereabouts. About ten days later—true to his vacillating treatment of us children—Dad returned with presents and then took us children home. I guess he figured that by then Mom would have "learned her lesson." I just had no earthly idea what "lesson" he had in mind.

Sorry as they were, some of Dad's tricks were also just a bit comical. I learned from the owner of the local fish market that he had once allowed Dad to hide in his fish freezer so he could elude the sheriff. The only problem was that the man had gotten busy enough to forget that he had more than fish in the freezer. When he finally remembered Dad, he hurried to the freezer to find out whether or not he had a frozen corpse on his hands. Thankfully, he didn't.

Probably the only reason Dad hadn't turned into exactly that was because the whiskey in his blood had kept his body temperature from dipping low enough to permit that to happen.

It's hardly any wonder that I felt quite insecure and fearful. I lived with frequent violence and a dad who was constantly in trouble with the law. But in

1959 when revival swept through our little community, my dad was one of the many men deeply affected. Suddenly, Dad was a changed man. He stopped drinking and swearing. I was there at the river the day he got baptized. I was in the church the night he stood and reflected upon his salvation experience.

Our family life greatly improved. We began going to church together. We enjoyed good wholesome entertainment together. Often after church services were over, we hurried home for a family time of watching Bonanza, a weekly popular TV program. We also enjoyed clean western movies and some of their actors, such as the Cartwrights, Roy Rogers and Dale Evans. *Leave It To Beaver, I Love Lucy,* and *Dennis the Menace* also ranked high.

There had been other brief periods of family mending. There had also been other times Dad had refrained from the bottle. This time, however, Dad seemed to have found peace. I too, began to relax—just a little.

Walter Allen Croom

3   Good 'Ole Mom

Truth was that by the time I was ten years of age, I was almost afraid of my own shadow and had turned myself into a literal "bundle of nerves." But there was always Mom, and it was to her that I looked for calm in the middle of my emotional storms.

Brown-haired and blue-eyed, Mom carried her five-feet-nine inches of height with the regal dignity and grace of the English stock from which she had descended. Age little dimmed her beauty of body and person. She walked with her shoulders back and her head held high. She never fancied herself better than anyone else, but neither did she give anyone an opportunity to patronize or look down on her. Her compliments were sincere—straight from the heart.

Like the rest of us, Mom enjoyed little of this world's goods, but never did she seek what she wanted by flattering someone or by allowing them to unnecessarily provide for her. Rather than sacrifice an ounce of her personal dignity by asking for a "handout," she "did without." If it proved necessary to ask for someone's help and that person was less than enthusiastic, Mom just never again asked. Wherever possible, Mom provided for herself. There was always a dollar in her pocket—just in case "things got tight," or she and the children needed "taxi fare to a safer place." Perhaps Mom had resolutely and blindly willed herself to believe that maybe someday someone or something might help her husband recapture the native graciousness that had attracted her to him. She had met him one evening in the mid-1930's when her brother Tommy had come home for a visit and had brought along with him Walter Ray Croom, with whom he lived and worked in the C. C. Camp that President Franklin D. Roosevelt's Great Depression recovery program had built along Highway 17 between Jacksonville and Maysville. Their friendship had blossomed, and in 1939, when they were both twenty-one years of age, they had been married.

At one time Dad must have cared deeply for Mom. But he had voluntarily chosen the bottle and it had robbed him of his kindness and thoughtfulness. But had his post-drinking, "I'm-sorry" gifts meant he still loved her—in his own twisted way? Hopefully, using her as his dumping grounds had somehow inversely translated into some indication that he felt secure in her strength even though he had been so long unable to reverse his debilitating behavior. But even if he professed "salvation," would that change things?

Why Mom continued to "stick it out" was perhaps a question that others asked. Perhaps she even asked it of herself. If such a question demanded an answer, Mom's response was that her children needed her. I certainly did.

Perhaps as helpful as Mom's self-sacrificing and emotional defense of us kids were her one-liners. Somehow, they held more punch, more sway than the few good ones Dad occasionally shared. Sometimes Mom's gems were quotes from Scripture, other times adages from old Ben Franklin, occasionally just hand-me-down family favorites. I suppose, though, that there was more truth bound up in those one-liners than in some entire textbooks.

"Son, if you lay down with dogs, you will get up with fleas" rescued me from questionable teen friendships. "The bed you make is the bed you sleep in" warned me not to drop out of high school. "A bird in the hand is better than two in the bush" challenged my change of jobs just to make more money. Of course, I soon discovered the wisdom of her few words and scurried back to my old job,

Much later in life, Mom's "where there's a will, there's a way" encouraged me to start—and finish—paying college bills. Of course, I wouldn't forget Mom's sacrificing—always doing things for us children—that occasionally put five-dollar bills in my college mailbox.

Now that I think about it, it was at every critical point in my life that I found Mom—just like a fresh rose with all its fragrance—striving to brighten up the world we lived in. If she hadn't, I'm afraid I might have figured out some easy way to check out. I knew such short brief interludes between panics.

Walter Allen Croom

4 Bottled Bondage

The freshness of Dad's 1959 "salvation" experience soured quite quickly. Working for up to a month at a time in other towns, he was just too far from Christian fellowship to sustain the profession he had made. It wasn't long before he returned home smelling like the bottle he had hoped to abandon.

Mother called for the pastor, who brought along several deacons. They joined Dad in the bedroom for prayer. Later, when I asked Dad about it, his solitary, sad reply was "Son, I'm sick." I didn't figure there was much question about that. And we both knew that he meant more than ordinary sickness. It was just much too clear that he was the artist's rendition of Solomon's words:

> Who has woe...? Who has redness of eyes...? Those who go in search of mixed wine...At last it bites like a serpent...Your eyes will see strange things...Your heart will utter perverse things. Yes, you will be like the one who lies down in the midst of the sea, or like the one who lies at the top of the mast saying, "They have struck me, but I did not feel it. When shall I awake, that I may seek another drink?" (Proverb 23:29-35)

Occasionally, Dad wept uncontrollably as he stared at some television evangelist sharing the gospel message. I suppose he was quite sorry that he had ever taken that first drink. Now he was proving what another old evangelist had said: "Sin takes you further than you want to go, keeps you longer than you want to stay and charges you more than you are willing to pay."

But, embarrassed, proud, and not wanting to admit that he was in trouble, Dad just packed us up and moved us—this time up a familiar old dirt road to a familiar old house owned by my granddad.

It was 1961, only one year after my Dad's supposed conversion. I was twelve years of age, and therefore had no way to defend myself against the consequences of Dad's actions. Moving—again—meant saying good-bye to my fishing buddy Steve, giving up my after-school paper delivery job, and enrolling in a school I didn't want to attend. About all I could do in self-defense was to trail Mom even more, swallow my anger and hurt, and keep my thoughts to myself.

There was no way I could have understood the workings of Dad's mind or even the motivations for his self-defeating actions. I don't think he could either. I had yet to develop my later love for biographies, so I did not yet know that God had dried up drunken lawyer Sam Jones and turned him into a loved Southern evangelist. Or gotten tippling Kansas State Attorney, C. I. Scofield, off his knees and nudged him to edit the Scofield Reference Bible. Or transformed a thoroughly shackled Mel Trotter from a father who had sold his child's shoes for drink into the man known for his founding fifty mission outreach programs. So I just agonized over why my dad didn't "get victory." Didn't he really want victory or had drinking gotten such an unbreakable grip on him that even salvation wouldn't loosen it?

Whatever the answer, my reality was limited to Granddad's farm and Dad's drinking. The first was okay. Granddad had two farms, one he had purchased in 1933, the other in 1934. The one on which we lived was very quiet. Often about the only two vehicles or people we saw in the course of a day were the mailman's vehicle and the school bus. The only other people I interacted with were new friends I eventually made in the community and my grandparents.

The second reality—Dad's drinking—was turning into a nightmare. Dad was no longer near the church and accountability. His drinking only increased, and with it came more violence. I remember awakening on Mother's Day 1962 and seeing my mother's face so badly beaten that I could hardly recognize her.

Then, in the month of July, Dad really lost it. It was a bad scene. Dad was drunk—again. His violence was cranking up—again. Everyone stayed out of the house—away from Dad. But when Dad came out, things turned super bad. He took a board and knocked my older brother, Donald on the head, then broke out the windows of his car. Blood gushing from his wound, Donald managed to make it to my uncle's place for help. Later, for some unknown reason, Dad took off after my two-year-old brother Danny. Danny had been Dad's pride and joy. There was Dad running incoherently across the yard waving an ax in Danny's direction. Danny was screaming at the top of his voice. I was frightened out of my wits, sure Dad was not even aware of what he was doing.

Of course, Dad ended up in jail for all of that, but several days later when Mom and my banged-up brother were in the courthouse appealing Dad's earlier court order to block payment of Donald's wages, Dad happened onto them and asked them to "take him home."

On the way back to the farmhouse, Dad asked if "Baby," as he called the three-month old, had any milk. When they arrived at the house, Dad asked Mom to come inside to see the new pots and pans that had just arrived. Mom knew better. She knew it was a ploy to entice her in so Dad could either make up or attack her, so she refused. He had gone too far this time. He had attacked her children.

Dad got out of the car and Mom and Donald drove off down the road. Things were in a sad state of affairs:

Donald had no car windows.

Danny was Dad's potential hostage. Mom feared Dad might "take him away."

And I couldn't erase the image of that ax.

 **5**

Fears and Fantasies

Dad was gone—for how long we couldn't know. Mom really feared, as did the rest of us, that Dad might just carry out the threat he had held over Mom for much too long—to return and "take Danny away." So she did what seemed the most logical thing to do. She moved us all in with her mother.

It was the summer of 1962, but the warmth outside hardly matched the chill in our hearts. Like my mother and siblings, I went to bed anxious, I woke up the same way. There was a warrant out for Dad's arrest, so if he did reappear, I knew he would likely be apprehended.

Keeping myself occupied was the best thing I could do, so I worked for my cousin who paid me $20.00 to pull potato sprouts and do other odd jobs. Two of those dollars I put into the offering plate at the nearby church we attended. The rest I gave to Mom so she could purchase groceries for us.

Summer came and went and Dad had not returned. He had not called. He had not written. No one told us they had seen him or even heard anything about him. So back to the little weatherboard house on Granddad's farm our smaller family went.

I spent a lot of time thinking about Dad. There were plenty of bad times to mull over, but I determined not to do that. I reviewed all the good times I could, convincing myself that if Dad was really gone, he had chosen to leave as an act of love. I figured he felt that if he were not with us, we would have fewer problems. He apparently knew that since he couldn't lick that drinking problem, he should simply leave.

That was probably nothing but wishful thinking on my part. But I was hurting and such rationalizations relieved the pain just a little. It also allowed me to keep holding on to the hope that if he had done something as painful as to leave us for a while because he loved us, he certainly didn't intend to forever abandon us.

I tried to escape loneliness—and check out what was going on in the world—by attaching myself to my transistor radio. John Glenn made me proud to be an American as he became the first one to orbit the earth. But when the news continually focused on how close Cuba and missiles brought us to nuclear war with Russia, I became quite uneasy. I had had enough of that kind of threat already. Bomb shelter signs plastered the halls of our school, and The White House and the Kremlin kept peppering the news with their threatening words and gestures. Maybe I'd never even get to grow up.

One way to make the time I might be allowed on this earth at least a little more enjoyable was to do something for myself. So I built a small one-room log cabin in the woods and made it my private hideaway. On occasion I attended Sunday school at the old abandoned one room hominy swamp school house. A lay preacher conducted services for the unchurched children in the area. I also went rabbit hunting whenever I could afford bullets for my gun. But I didn't just turn myself into a hermit. I also occasionally rode my bike into town and hung out.

Perhaps one reason I didn't retreat into a private shell was because I began noticing the other gender.

Just down the road from where we lived was a young girl by the name of Linda. I managed to make her my first sweetheart, even practicing my first kiss with her. The only problem was that just a little further down the road lived my friend Dwight, and he and I knew some friendly contention for Linda's affection.

Linda's attentions, notwithstanding, there were other things that also attracted me. Hanging out one day in town, I overheard two older men discussing how to make homemade wine, so I listened in and memorized the recipe. I could hardly wait to get home and try it out. Of course, I needed grapes, but that was no problem since in the woods down the road from us was an orchard of wild grapes. I felt sure that they were mine for the taking since all that could be seen around them was an old foundation on which a house had once stood. No house, no people, no problem. Someone had abandoned those grapes and they were there for me. I knew that each autumn those vines literally hung heavy with grapes, so I picked several buckets full and, using my overheard recipe, whipped up several jars of grape wine. Up in the attic went those jars, and there they stayed until they had fully fermented. It didn't occur to me at the time that that may have been exactly how Dad had headed in the direction he had.

Of course, I balanced out my activities with some quite commendable activities, like a spelling bee, for example. Yet I didn't last long. I was the second person to misspell a word and have to sit down. Only then did I discover that I had studied the wrong list of words. But mistake or not, that spelled failure for me.

For some reason, failure followed me in other pursuits too. My homemade banjo turned out an absolute flop. Then I failed the seventh grade. I had already been there, done that in first grade, so I decided I'd had enough of failure and I determined to drop out of school. Nobody would let me do that though for the simple reason that I was only fourteen. So, since nobody would let me stop school, I decided to just stop studying.

I began to dream big dreams. Fantasize may have been the better word. I would be a rock star. Hardly expecting such would ever be the case, I in this way kept my mind busy enough to maintain some semblance of sanity. I even gave up the smoking habit I had picked up as an experimenting thirteen-year-old. I was hardly concerned about tobacco. Most of the farmers in our area made their living by growing the stuff, and most of the church buildings were constructed from the proceeds of tithing tobacco farmers. I quit smoking because it made me feel weak and dizzy. Almost any physical problem caused me to think about dying prematurely, and I didn't need that to think about. Dad's absence—creeping past a year—had carved out of my life a bigger hole than I dared admit. I still could not call it abandonment.

There were two persons, however, who helped fill just a little of that void. They were my granddad and his second wife who lived just down the road from our house. They were quite the oasis in the desert of my parched young life.

The granddad I knew was a sweet and understanding little old man who stood about five feet-seven-inches tall, weighed about one hundred ten pounds soaking wet, and had just a little white hair left around his ears. The granddad I knew was a kind and gentle man. Never once did I hear a foul word from his lips. He constantly talked about Jesus, his favorite line being "Bless the Lord, Bud." At 75,

Granddad still worked circles around everyone I knew. Whenever I spent the night at his place, he would awaken me about 5:30 a.m. to help him get ready for the day of harvest before the local hired laborers arrived. We would work through the day up until the sun began to set. After the "hired hands" checked out for the day, I would retire to Granddad's large bathtub for a comfortable soak while Granddad "readied" things for the following day. After he had eaten supper, taken a bath and gone to bed, I lay in my bed and listened in on his overly loud praying. The neighborhood claim was that he could be heard way down that country road!

I found Granddad's wife—Mrs. Hood as she was called—just as loveable even though some felt uncomfortable that she had married Granddad so soon after Grandma's death. Many hours I spent pulling weeds from this step-grandmother's flower gardens. And just as often she would call me into the house for apple pie and a glass of milk at her kitchen table. I never opened up to her and she never pressed me about what was going on in my life. Yet she seemed to be able to look deep within my soul and see my hurt and pain. After a nice long chat it was back to the yard and the flowers. But in our time together I had sensed her understanding and felt her comfort. Her radiant face warmed my chilled heart.

Truth was, though, that things had not always been that way. I learned that Granddad had known the same alcoholic start in life as had my dad. But Granddad had tried to hide it. In fact, once when he was a small boy, one of my father's brothers had found his dad's liquor bottle hidden in the barn and had drunk so much of it he couldn't walk straight. The poor little fellow escaped a spanking only because someone else in the family reminded Granddad that that bottle was his and that if he didn't want his son to get drunk, he should have kept it out of sight better!

But try to hide it or not, such things refuse to stay hidden, and though at age sixty, Granddad had committed his life to God and had lost the alcohol habit, it had already tempted two of his sons into a lifestyle that eventually took their lives. Two other of his children had moved out of state and were not heard from for many years, and one grandchild died of a drinking related disease.

But, nice as it was to live near Granddad, the day came when we moved from that depressing little farmhouse near him and went back to a house on the "half moon." I found that place quiet and peaceful. There I could work for local farmers during the summer months so that I could buy school clothes. There I was close enough to hitchhike or catch a ride over to Richlands on Saturday evenings for lessons on a form of square dancing called clogging.

One Saturday evening, it was raining when our lessons were finished, and the square dance instructor offered to take me home. When we got near the cut-off road that led to my house I said, "I live just a little ways down this road" and got out to walk the remaining mile. As soon as the car was out of sight, I took off my shoes, rolled up my pants legs and walked down that muddy road. By the time I reached home, the mud was firmly packed between my toes and I was soaking wet. For some reason, even though this house was nicer looking than any other of our houses, I was embarrassed for anyone to see it. I wanted people to think only the best of me.

I guess I so wanted to "belong" that I was willing to do things to make that happen. Even educator John

Dewey and child-care specialist Dr. Benjamin Spock were then advocating self-expression and individualism. The Beetles had captured the fancy of more than one nation that way—growing long hair and plucking a guitar along with songs like "I Wanna Hold Your Hand" and "She Loves You, Yea, Yea, Yea!" But my hair wouldn't cooperate very quickly, so I hurried things up by buying and wearing a wig—at the appropriate times. I also purchased my first guitar, a Sears-style Silvertone.

Music became my diversion, my obsession. I had figured out a way to ignore the realities around me. Perhaps I could forget that though Martin Luther King, Jr.'s August, 1963, "I Have A Dream" speech offered hope, people were burning flags or pushing mass demonstrations, like the one in Birmingham, to near riot. With that guitar in hand, I could pretend to be any rock star or famous recording artist I wished to be. There was some kind of imaginary security in that imaginary world of writing music and playing in nightclubs.

I hadn't lost my desire to drop out of school, but until I could find a job, I knew better than to do that. So in the summer of 1965, when I was seventeen, I decided to hop on a Trailways bus to Louisiana and spend time with my sister. I hoped I would not be unnecessarily detained by the over-frequent marches and demonstrations in Southern cities.

Really, it wasn't only the South that was restless. Earlier in the year, New York had seen the assassination of Black Nationalist Malcolm X. Riots in Watts had left thirty-four people dead and had sparked ghetto riots in several other places. So if President Lyndon B. Johnson's "Great Society" hadn't helped all that much at home, would his authorized offensive operations fare any better in South Vietnam?

Fortunately, I made it to Louisiana okay, moved in with my sister, Charlotte, and found a job at Duplantis Motor Company in Morgan City. It was great to get to know a sister I was barely acquainted with. I even enjoyed my job washing cars and running errands. Of course, the nice part was making money and being able to "putt around" in the company car.

Since my sister, Charlotte, was attending a Southern Baptist Church in the area, I tagged along. There I heard enough to again fall under conviction. I dedicated my life to the Lord and vowed to do His will. The only thing I really hesitated giving over to Him completely was my music.

At the end of the summer, I knew—for the first time since I was 14—that I really did want to finish school. Believe it or not, I was even elected treasurer of my high school class. Life seemed a bit on the mend. That was until one evening when I received a telephone call from my sister who said she had learned of an opening on the boat where her husband worked. What she added tempted me. "If you take the job, you can also do night classes and pick up your G.E.D." To a seventeen-year-old boy, the offer looked great. It looked like both good money and a great opportunity to finish my education on the side. I hopped the first plane out of town, convinced that this was my lucky break. After a few days at sea, however, I realized that I had a big problem. The only place I was comfortable was on my back. Even the sight of water nauseated me. About all I could do was heave and heave until nothing more would come up. I thought I'd die if we didn't soon reach land. As soon as we hit dry land, I hurried to my sister's house to try to sleep it off. The following morning, I was just as sick and had to literally brace myself against the walls to walk even a few steps. Sis' husband, Houston, had left for work but soon called to say that the boat was going to Texas. I sure wished I could go, but I knew better, so right then and there I quit and went back to that earlier summer job of washing cars and running errands for Duplantis Motor Company.

Yes, I had failed. But, no, I wasn't a quitter. At least I didn't think I was. Yet, one afternoon while I was washing cars, my head began to shake, my heart pounded with fear, and my limbs began to tremble as my whole emotional world unraveled. I knew something abnormal was going on, so in an unthinking, desperate attempt to stop shaking, I began to shove into my mouth some of the soap I was using to clean cars. But all at once it occurred to me that soap, even its frothy bubbles, might be poisonous, so I began spitting them up.

Every night after that, I looked forward to going to bed just so my head would stop shaking. But when I awoke, that annoying bodily tic started all over again. Whatever was going on I didn't know. All I knew was that I was 1,000 miles from home, a high school dropout and stuck in a dead-end job with no hope of advancement. Was I experiencing a breakdown? Would I lose my mind?

My sister was a wonderful person, but she wasn't Mom, and Mom wasn't here. I had no security—or maybe I should say—no security blanket. So out came that good old guitar. In the privacy of my sister's home with that guitar on my lap, I knew just a little bit of relief. There I knew no pain, and I could imagine everything turning out right. There, since I was the good guy, I wouldn't lose. But of course, I had to get up every morning and go back out to that real world of washing cars, too. And since I wanted to purchase a car, I prolonged my day by taking on an evening job. But since that left little time for youth functions at church, I began to lose vital contacts with Christians and began to slip away from fellowship with the Lord. And then one evening on my way to my second job, because I began to distractedly stare at two girls in the rear view mirror, I slammed my sister's car into the back of the car in front of me. The best thing I knew to do was to notify my employers that I was quitting, pack my bags, and go back home.

There I again obsessed on my one solace—music. Perhaps if I practiced continually, I could get a job in a local nightclub. Then I would have money, acceptance...I felt like an animal driven by some intense hunger—in my case—hunger for peace. I was a believer—I even prayed every night before going to bed, but my soul was a desert. I wished for a giant shoulder, for wide-open arms...for whoever or whatever would make those crushing fears and anxieties subside.

I was five when this picture was taken.
Which one am I ?

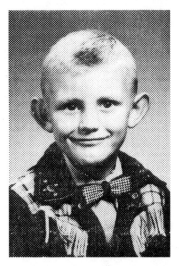

Age 6

Age 16

1969 From left to right
First row Ralph, Danny, Charlotte
Second row Walter, Mother, Phil, Donald

Tracing my steps to the old tennant farm house located
on the Marshburn farm.

Walter Allen Croom

6 Hamburgers and Hangups

Whenever I got a few dollars together, I headed for Bob's Bar and Grill for the best hamburgers around—fresh ground hamburger simmered on the grill, draped with cheese, sizzled some more, then lifted onto a fresh bun, and served with lettuce, tomato, onions and a Coke. Just 25 cents! But hamburgers were only part of the reason I found Bob's so attractive. No, it wasn't the bar that lined one side of the grill. That I never patronized. Rather, it was the poolroom located at the rear of the building. There my good friend, Bobby Lovitt, and I spent many hours shooting pool. While we shot, Bobby and I would pop coins into the jukebox and listen to such songs as Roy Orbison's "Pretty Woman" or a Beetles' or Elvis Presley hit. As a form of "heavenly" relief, that ranked next to playing my guitar.

Mom knew I had flip-flopped back and forth in my spiritual walk since I was eleven. She recognized that I was treating my salvation more like an insurance policy than a relationship and I might easily tip towards a life of sin, so she nudged me in the direction of more spiritual interests. Quite the wise woman, she invited me to the small country church she attended with "There's a lot of nice looking girls over there."

"Girls," I thought, swallowing her timely bait. "Let's go."

The very first Sunday I was there, several young people encouraged me to come back. Their encouragement did the trick, and I began developing new friendships. One of the most special was with a young lady by the name of Judy K. Morton. That fifteen-year-old, with her brown hair and cute little dimples, was the prettiest thing I had seen in a very long time. It took me a while, but I finally screwed up enough courage to talk to her, and finding her agreeable to my attentions, I visited at her home several times until her folks—complying with the local custom of early dating and marriage—consented to our double dating with another couple.

Judy was the middle birth child of three in the family of Cyrus and Margaret Morton. With her parents, she lived next to the small Ma and Pa country grocery store and meat market her father had established along the Piney Green Highway just northeast of Jacksonville, North Carolina, after having worked up through a similar establishment in his youth. A special treat was that she was a believer, having found Christ as her Savior in a Billy Graham tent revival.

Of course, I found Judy the main attraction of the family, but I did really also appreciate getting to know her parents, especially her father who always seemed to be smiling. Having grown up on the farm during the depression years, Cyrus might have had plenty of "hard time" stories to share, but his favorite were war stories. He had enrolled for a two-year overseas hitch in the Army—Hawaii—but because World War II had begun just six months after he enlisted, he remained in uniform for four and one-half years. When he began one of his tales, his wife Margaret protested by quietly walking out of the room. I listened with interest. One story I enjoyed was how Japanese bombers had only mildly disturbed Cyrus' morning smoke on the doorsteps of the military mess where he was a cook the morning they bombed Pearl Harbor. He and the other fellows had at first figured that bombers overhead signaled only a drill. But he had seen plenty of action after that. In fact, he had survived hand-to-hand combat and had had the misfortune of watching almost his entire platoon lose their lives. His theater of war covered the Philippines, the Guadalcanal, and the New Hebrides Islands, and he had spent some time in New Zealand recovering from battle wounds.

Perhaps it was Cyrus' several close encounters with death that had given him his profound appreciation for life. That endeared him to me for it was obvious that he had something I obviously did not. He was at peace with both His maker and himself, and I was a perennial bundle of nerves. Like my granddad, Cyrus had drunk and smoked and, in fact, even sold alcohol right alongside of his groceries. It was not until the 1960's that he had become a believer in Christ. Although after that he had stopped drinking and shortly thereafter stopped selling alcohol in his store, he had continued to smoke—a quite common habit among Southern Christians—serving as both a deacon and a Sunday School teacher in the church where we all attended.

Pastor J. V. Johnson, a wise and practical man, asked me whether I would be willing to count those who attended Sunday School and then post that number on the attendance and hymn register that hung in the church auditorium. Saturday nights, I often stayed "out with the guys" until the wee hours of the morning, but I always managed to get to church on time to take care of that task. Had not Rev. Johnson wisely involved me in that little responsibility, I likely would have become a church dropout. But having been so "needed," I determined to faithfully execute that small duty.

Whatever sense of obligation may have been involved, I regularly attended church and so was benefitted by the consistent preaching of God's Word. At the end of a week of revival meetings—May 22, 1966—I dedicated my life to the Lord—again. I say again because I had earlier "walked the aisle" in a tent service where my cousin was preaching and again during a service when I was in Louisiana visiting my sister.

This time the speaker was Bobby Jackson, a famed Freewill Baptist minister, but it was not his reputation that drew me. This time I was placing a marker in my life by responding to the evangelist's thought provoking challenge, "If Communists overran the church this morning, would you take a stand for Christ? Would you be willing to die for Him?" As the song leader stepped to the pulpit and began to lead the congregation in several stanzas of "Just As I Am," I nearly ran to the altar. I was broken over my back-slidden Christian walk and I wanted cleansing, forgiveness, and, this time, God's peace.

After Evangelist Bobby Jackson had moved on, it was to Pastor Johnson that I turned for help. A farmer like his father before him, Pastor Johnson may have appeared an unlikely candidate for the job of helping me move from fear to faith. He had had neither university nor seminary training and probably could not have discussed much about any religion other than Christianity. Nor was he well armed to combat the religious trends of the day. He knew that even three-time Presidential candidate William Jennings Bryan and his famous Dayton, Tennessee "monkey trials" had failed to keep the ACLU and their

New York lawyer, Clarence Darrow, from railroading Darwin's hundred-year-old evolutionary ideas into almost every public school curriculum in the nation. Yet that undaunted Rev. Johnson just kept on unapologetically and stubbornly preaching that the Bible was the Word of God.

Pastor Johnson never insisted that the Bible was a science text, but he did insist that wherever the Bible addressed matters of science, its statements were correct. After all, its writers had written under the inspiration of the Holy Spirit, so how could they have made faulty scientific statements? So would he quibble over the difference between a stone and a fossil? Hardly. Worry whether the sun sets or the earth rises? Hardly. Run from the higher critics who argue that Jonah wasn't swallowed by a whale? Hardly. As Rev. Johnson put it, "If God can create a world out of nothing, he certainly can create a large fish out of something."

Rev. Johnson just didn't seem to need scientific explanations for much of anything. As he saw it, all truth was God's truth no matter where it was found. But, in matters of faith and practice, the Bible was the final authority "the standard by which we [were to] evaluate everything." Rev. Johnson also was incurably convinced that though the Bible was not a history text, its historical statements and accounts were historically accurate. Believing that God had both created the world and given His precious Son to redeem the world seemed quite enough. After all, his life had been changed by the power of the gospel, and others were experiencing the same thing.

That was certainly true. Nearly every week those church doors were open, people received Christ as their personal Savior. Rev. Johnson had done nothing more than insist on one thing—that Jesus was the eternal Son of God and that the Book from which he preached was God's inerrant and infallible Word which teaches us both how to get to heaven and how to experience life with the quality of heaven in it.

As I took in more and more of God's word, I too began to affirm the authority of the Bible as the Word of God for my life. Fear had too long been my god, I had too long listened to the voice of fear. I had granted it more authority than the Scriptures. Now, I intended to believe my way out of fear, but I still felt I needed something to hold onto. That, Rev. Johnson assured me, was the Christ of Scripture as seen in God's Holy Word.

So that I could stay close to God's special revelation to me, I tucked a New Testament into my pocket and made use of it every spare moment I could grab while cleaning offices, answering phones, cutting grass, and running documents between the courthouse and the law firm of my employers, Ellis, Hooper, Warlick, and Waters.

One day while I was waiting in the courthouse to pick up some legal papers, a lady complimented me on studying a pocket dictionary. I was still too shy to tell her that it was no dictionary—that it was the words of Jesus—but I did manage the courage to take time during my lunch hour to walk down to the nursing home and spend quick minutes with some of the older residents. One dear lady who saw me so addicted to the Scriptures suggested that I might become a bit unbalanced by reading nothing more than the Bible. Little did she know that I was already quite unbalanced; I was already a literal roller coaster of emotions. So, although I appreciated her genuine concern for me, I reminded myself that I was accessing something that could give me clear-cut answers and could stabilize my wobbly life. I was merely helping myself to the Truth so the Truth could "set me free"—free in spirit.

As I continued to read the Scripture and make practical application, I began noticing I felt more frequent and longer periods of peace and liberty. Sure, there were still definite bouts with fear and anxiety, but I was moving toward my goal. And if that dear old lady's concern mattered, as I reached beyond the Scriptures, even those sources pointed me back to God. Fulfilled prophecies reinforced my belief in Scripture. Checking out what archeologists had dug up provided proof that God knew what He was talking about. Even the Dead Sea Scrolls had made it abundantly clear that our Bible was the same Bible the early church had used. I had found a resource I could trust in and refer to. The Bible had now become my foundation, and as I turned my attentions from trying to stand on that foundation to enjoying its firmness beneath me, my life was slowly changing.

I guess one of the first things I became convinced of—finally—was that not even Mom could be my security. She had long been that—my calm in the eye of my storms—but that scary breakdown in Louisiana had begun the nagging awareness that not even she could be my inner strength. As I began to accept God's Word for what it was—God's word—I noticed that music was losing its death grip on my life. Oh, I still played my guitar—and really enjoyed doing just that—but I no longer felt obsessed with the dream of playing in nightclubs. Rather, I accompanied as Judy and I sang in our local church. Before long, we were receiving invitations to play and sing elsewhere as well.

As I continued to read God's Word, I noticed the Holy Spirit putting his finger on living and thinking patterns my past life had thrived on. I had never really paid much attention to my motivations. Now I realized that my disposition of fear had long excused convenient lying. For example, when I had applied to work for the law firm, I had told Mr. Hooper, my interviewer, that I had dropped out of high school in the twelfth grade. That was a lie. I had also told him I had never been involved in an accident. That was a lie. I knew I had said such things because I had been too fearful, too afraid of consequence, to own up to truth. But now Scripture, not others' opinions, was my standard of conduct, and I knew I needed to "put away lying" and "put on truth". I had never before confessed to any wrongdoing. It was a bit scary, but I just told my boss the truth about things and said I was sorry. On the other side of his office door, I sighed with relief never even remotely aware that he might decide to fire me. I was just too concerned about being right with God. (Perhaps that's why he later gave me a check to process my college application).

There was one problem though. My addiction to Bob's Bar and Grill hamburgers had long before rubbed off on my boss, Mr. Hooper. But now I felt I couldn't run hamburger errands anymore. Oh, the hamburgers were still as tempting, but now I had decided to pass them up rather than keep on trying to not notice the alcohol of the bar, the sickening smoke of the poolroom, and the betting of the men who frequented the place. God's Word seemed to be telling me that such places were not conducive to spiritual growth. And, I must confess that I was fearful that if anyone from the local church saw me frequenting that place, they would not think well of my Christian walk. One day when Mr. Hooper sent me down to Bob's to get him one of those great hamburgers, I came back with a hamburger from a local fast food stop. I hoped he wouldn't notice the difference. Big chance for that! Mr. Hooper just took one look at it and slammed it on the desk, super angry.

Sure, I was trying to rid my life of unhealthy associations and practices that I felt the Scriptures were bringing to my attention. But I still didn't realize the emotional baggage I was trying to lug around. It was terrible trying to juggle the expectations of others with the needless baggage cluttering my emotions. That annoying bodily tic plagued my movements. So did obsessive compulsive behaviors. If I scratched one hand, I felt compelled to scratch the other, fearful that something horrible might happen if I did not obey whatever inner voice prompted me to follow certain rituals. Many nights after going to bed, I got up to check or recheck the door locks, the kitchen stove...Something inside kept nagging, "God doesn't love you. You're not worthy of being loved." Yet, though I eventually recognized that such thoughts were not God's thoughts, I felt even more accused of so accusing God. Sometimes, I felt so shaken, I grabbed my head and just tried to slow its shaking, hoping that outer stillness might help settle the inward turmoil. "God, why is this happening?" I screamed more to myself than to God.

Of course, such struggles only added to my already unhealthy self-consciousness. I had been blessed with an over-abundance of ear, and, as a child, had often been singled out by other children. My own mother had even once wondered out loud about having my ears pinned back. I had known she had meant no harm, but I had definitely personalized her comment and had concluded that even she had a problem with those things God had given me to hear others with. Not far from those offensive ears were my teeth. They needed serious work, so rarely did I allow myself to smile. Of course, I couldn't talk with my mouth shut, but what came out of it needed work too. My grammar and diction were atrocious. I sat on a "cheer" rather than a chair. I drove a car that ran on "tars" rather than tires. I had worked in the "bacca" field. I enjoyed eating "matoes" and "taters."

Quite convinced that I was hardly a candidate for realizing many of my dreams of self-improvement, I was thoroughly shocked one day when, during my lunchtime Scripture reading, I came across Philippians 4:13. As I read its literal words, "I can do all things through Christ who strengthens me," I got so excited I nearly fell out of my seat. If what that verse said was actually true, maybe I could actually see my dreams come true. Perhaps I could have victory over my personal difficulties. But could I really finish my high school education, even eventually go to college? Yet, wasn't that what that verse seemed to imply?

Up to this point, I had felt nothing but failure. I had failed the first grade and the seventh grade. I had failed in a spelling bee. I had dropped out of school. I could point to no positive accomplishments. Yet the one thing I wanted more than anything else was success. Did I dare dream that might sometime happen?

I had acted out failure because I had believed I was and would continue to be a failure. I had no idea that if I wanted to bring my runaway emotions under control, I needed to confront my negative thinking processes. Feeling right could only follow thinking right. But what I did seem to find in that short verse was the suggestion that I could do things because Christ would energize me.

That suggestion, those possibilities, followed me the rest of that day. Over and over I reflected on those good words, "I can do all things through Christ who strengthens me." They slowly became a springboard forward. They moved me from reverse into drive. They became the impetus for me to put one foot squarely in front of the other and begin to move in the direction of my dreams. I continued to date Judy and to attend the small country church led by Pastor Johnson. I also enrolled in a G.E.D. program, attending classes two evenings a week.

Walter Allen Croom

 # 7

Rattled

On February 26, 1967, Judy and I teamed up. That is, we were married—she at sixteen and I at eighteen. Really, we were "children" with no earthly idea what a Christ-centered marriage was all about. Judy's role model of marriage and family was obviously better than mine, but neither of us had had any pre-marital counseling, nor did we know any such thing might even be available.

Our physical assets were meager too. My car had just sputtered its last, so I borrowed my father-in-law's car and made a quick overnight trip for a honeymoon. The following day we were back in our little two-bedroom house on Cox avenue in Jacksonville, North Carolina, a place close enough for me to walk back and forth to work at that familiar law firm of Ellis, Hooper, Warlick and Waters as well as to continue my GED evening classes.

What I most enjoyed was studying the Scripture and attending our local church. As I continued to sit under the preaching of the Word, I soon became interested in sharing the Gospel message. My pastor, recognizing something positive was taking place in my life, one day threw out another challenge. "Walter Allen," he said, "Would you like to preach this coming Wednesday night?" I hoped he knew the chance he was taking. What did I know? Not even the difference between the Saul of the Old Testament and the Saul of the New or between John the Baptist and John the

Beloved. But if my pastor had faith in me, I didn't want to let him down. He had no idea, though, how fearful I was. I had hardly yet moved beyond the kind of fear that makes the hands sweat, the heart palpitate, the mind block. Had he known, he may have foregone the invitation or taken me to his study for some fatherly wisdom. He certainly must have noticed my obvious, annoying nervous mannerisms. But if he had, he must also have decided that I could best develop poise and confidence by doing the very thing that seemed to bring on those actions—speaking in public. During the next several days, while I constantly referred to Philippians 4:13 for the strength, I worked diligently to put together a message. I practically wrote out my whole message (a practice I maintained for many years to control cloudy thoughts and rapid heartbeats). Wednesday night, my message lasted the whole way through ten minutes! Whatever Pastor Johnson thought, he at least kept on asking me to speak.

Pastor Johnson's confidence in me sparked a new dream in me. Now instead of trying to fulfill my childhood dream of becoming a well-known scientist or my teen aspirations toward music stardom, I fantasized about becoming a great evangelist or pastor. Good as the idea was, however it apparently grew out of my own sense of insecurity, so I slowly found myself propelled right back to the old patterns of tension and fear of failure.

Unfortunately, by the end of 1967 even my GED aspirations conspired against this new kind of success I had begun seeking. There were now one-half million troops in both Vietnams, and the 500th U.S. plane had been shot down over North Vietnam. I knew I would probably be exchanging GED classes for military drills. Sure, I was a patriotic American, but I wasn't excited about going off to war. Being drafted was synonymous with going to Vietnam and Nam was synonymous with dying. That was one thing I didn't want to do.

Aside from the bare fact that I wanted to go on living, I really did have serious doubts about the morality of such a war. The "victim" of a progressive John Dewey education, I had learned to question. And I did. I guess I did have questions why we as a nation could run the gamut of contradictions from forty-three dying in one of Detroit's worst race riots in history to Thurgood Marshall's being appointed as the first Black justice on the Supreme Court. Or why good deeds were buried in print while "life" for the Boston Strangler had to hit the headlines.

But answers to those questions didn't threaten me. They didn't affect my personal safety. What did though, was that awful war going on in a little country in Southeast Asia. For the first time in history, TV was bringing war into our living rooms. Every night there were Walter Cronkite, David Brinkley, and Chet Huntley with the horrors and bloodshed of a war that was going nowhere. Death in any form was horrible. Finding it at the hands of enemies we had no intentions of conquering was ridiculous. But neither could I bring myself to protest or march on the issue. There was enough of that. Even Jane Fonda and Michael Stokely were championing opposition movements such as the April 1967 Washington, D.C. anti-war protest.

But, maybe there was a legitimate way to avoid the draft. I wrote to a Bible College in Tennessee and requested permission to attend so I could answer a draft notice with a divinity student waiver. Mr.

Hooper, the boss who had forgiven both my Bob's hamburger stunt and my interviewing lying even gave me the money for the application. But the school wrote back requiring a high school equivalency diploma before doing college level work. A friend suggested that I become a conscientious objector, but after a short consideration, I decided I was too conscientious to pull that stunt. I'd have to go after the only other exemption I knew of—becoming a father-to-be. And would you believe that Selective Service changed my draft classification from I-A to 3-A when my dear wife verified her pregnancy.

I was grateful—to whom I wasn't sure. I had been petrified by the possibility of going to war. But I hadn't expected God to help me so conveniently out of my dilemma. In fact, I was almost ashamed of myself. To show God how much I appreciated His help, I decided to get back to those GED studies. However, one snowflaky March evening in 1968, Judy rattled me just a little too hard.

"Walt, something feels funny here," she complained, putting her hand on her slightly bulging middle. All of a sudden, I felt sick there too.

"Oh, no," I whispered more to myself than to God. "Don't let her miscarry."

All night Judy rolled with sharp pains. I tossed with sharper dread. I don't know which of us hurt worse in the morning when the doctor made it official. Judy had miscarried.

In a few days, Judy was back on her feet. But I was a wreck. No baby meant Vietnam. Why wouldn't it? There were half a million troops there by now. Even the war hawks were biting their fingernails over the two-billion-dollar-a-month hole this war was punching into the dollar. Now I was I-A again. I should say, *I* knew I was I-A again. The registration office didn't, but I also knew that I wouldn't be able to live with either myself or God if I didn't tell them.

It wasn't exactly fun to pull that post office door and walk past those "Your Country Needs You" posters to a little door marked "Registration Office," but, allowing the Bible to influence the decisions I made, I did it. No more would I lie just to keep things comfortable for me. If doing right came with a high price tag, that was the way it would be.

When I pulled the door of that registration office shut behind me, I was both relieved and upset. Should I take my chances on being drafted into the infantry? Or, should I beat that by signing up with the Air Force? Since my employers had suggested that the Air Force might be less of a risk than the draft, I reluctantly checked in with the recruiting officer. After an interview and testing, he promised me I'd get my Air Force blue if I chose to join. And I could leave in about two weeks.

For two tense weeks I debated. Join. Don't join. Don't join. Join. At the end of those two weeks, I had a tight stomach and no answer. When the phone rang and a business-like voice again invited me to join the "boys in blue," I prayed with my eyes open and said simply, "Thanks, but, No thanks." I could have mistaken the voice on the other end of the line for the little boy who had lost his candy. "If you don't join us, you'll be drafted."

"Thanks," I said surprisingly firm, "I'll take my chances." Blue was obviously safer than Army green, but it was a four-year hitch. That was two years more than I would have done in the Army. I didn't want to give two, much less four.

I have no way of knowing but I have a suspicion that the Air Force recruiter laid down his phone and walked across that post office lobby and handed the Army recruiter my name because within two weeks, just as I had supposed it would happen, I received an official invitation from the United States Army. But now that it had come, I was far less fearful than I had supposed I might have been. The only way I could explain that to myself was that I had begun to believe what God had said to David, "The Lord is the Strength of my life; of whom shall I be afraid?"

Soon after, on a May 1968 morning, I got to test out that promise. The hardest steps I ever took in my adult life were the few that led me from Judy to a dull green military bus. I was on my way to learn how to defend other people's freedoms, but I felt as though everything and everyone—even God—had literally pushed me into the very thing I had tried to dodge.

I dropped into a seat where I could spot Judy. The bus driver flopped into the driver's seat, shifted the transmission into reverse, then forward, and began pulling out into the street. I waved in the direction I knew Judy would be standing, but it was hard to see whether or not she returned my wave because my eyes were filling with tears. I wasn't about to let anyone see them spill over. "Jump off and go home with Judy," my heart screamed.

"Sit still and get busy," my head whispered.

I reached into my jacket and pulled out a little book I had brought along to keep me company. For the next one-and-a-half hours, I devoured page after page. I knew the chances I'd get at that New Testament for the next eight weeks would be few.

When I heard the bus choke to a stop, I blinked, tucked my New Testament back into my jacket and unwillingly uncurled from my cement seat. I climbed out and, with all the rest, disappeared into Fort

Bragg's Induction Center. In no time at all, like the rest of the guys, I was government issue right down to my underwear. I had donated most of my hair to the barber. And, I was no longer Walter Allen Croom; I was a serial number.

Somehow, I managed the rest of the day all right. That was just a lot more of the same thing. But it was night that got to me. Instead of my Serta Perfect, it was just a lumpy bunk in a barracks with bare floors, bare walls, bare windows. And, instead of Judy beside me, it was thirty-nine other just as homesick fellows who, for all I know, did what I did—buried my face in my pillow and quietly bawled like a baby.

A couple days of Fort Bragg style roll-up-your-sleeves, grab-those-tags, and we were off to "real" training. When the bus dropped us off outside Company C, there was Sgt. Robinson waiting for us. He certainly looked unpleasant, and he was like a hound dog after a rabbit, he ran us, duffel bags and all, from the bus to the barracks. Inside he lined us up twenty in a row. He paced up and down between the rows screaming volume after volume of unrememberable company policy. One little black fellow from Philadelphia made the childish mistake of snickering. Sgt. Robinson wheeled around wild-eyed, cursed the air blue, dashed a handy cigarette butt can half-filled with water right into Ronnie's face, and dared him to ever smile again.

The next day, and the next, and the...Sgt. Robinson repeated himself. He ranted. He screamed. He called us every name in the book and a few more he must have found somewhere else. Then when he had completely browbeaten us, he whipped us into shape. Chin-ups, marches, sit-ups, sprints. My soft civilian hands blistered raw, I discovered bones and muscles doctors must have overlooked. I could hardly stand straight up. But before long, I could salute, pivot, and work out as well as any other G.I. I could survive sun-up to sun-down and midnight guard duty tossed in, too. I had even gained weight!

But that's about where the benefits ended. My body was in better shape than it had ever been. But my mind sure wasn't. Combat training with its dummies, its bayonets, its kill...kill...kill brought back the worst of my fears. It was bad enough that I already knew that...

...North Korea was holding hostage the USS Pueblo's eighty-two crewmen.

...the Viet Cong had launched massive Tet offensives.

...Martin Luther King, Jr. had been murdered in Memphis.

...N. Y. Senator Robert F. Kennedy had been assassinated.

But heaped on top of all that was Sgt. Robinson's insinuation that anybody with "religion" wasn't worth the space he took up. None of it exactly encouraged me to turn to the Lord for the support I needed. Oh, I knew that I had the Lord with me and had Judy to pray for me. But, I couldn't feel it. So the Lord decided to let me look down from the top of a telephone pole at Fort Dix,

"Strap on those spikes," droned a tough Ft. Dix telecommunications instructor. I strapped them on. "Bury them in that pole," he continued. I did. "Now lean way back," he barked. I leaned—a little.

"Hand-over-hand-it-up-to-the-top," he barked. I managed five feet, ten feet..."Way back, you idiot," he snorted. "Whadja wanna do—fall?" NOOOO! That's why I'm hugging the pole. I leaned WAY back.

At the top, I unsteadily snapped the safety belt around my waist and the pole. I looked down. Below me—25 feet below me—was none-too-soft clay. Over to my right was an ambulance. I could just see my buddies scraping me up with the clay and hurrying the mess to the ambulance. Or, "Charlie" leaving me dangling from the top of one of his poles in Vietnam—dead.

"Perrrfect love casts out all feeear," I chattered.

"Perffect love casts out all feeaar," I begged.

"Perfect love casts out all fear," I scolded myself.

But still fear choked the rest of my stay there at Fort Dix. Fear that the next time I wouldn't make it up and down that pole. Fear that next would be Vietnam.

My Fort Dix graduation day was cool and sharp like October should be, but I was hot. Nineteen other fellows fell in with me for platoon inspection. Then we nervously re-grouped at our company. Out came the orders. I ripped mine open and gasped. Eleven of us had orders to Vietnam, six to someplace called Aberdeen Proving Grounds, three to somewhere else. I was one of the six ordered to Aberdeen.

As soon as I dared, I scooted off to the nearest pay phone. Judy had to be first to know. That high lasted the whole flight home for leave with Judy in North Carolina. I stepped off that airplane proud of the mosquito wing I'd just sewn on my new dress greens. It didn't take me long to spot a brown-haired gal I hadn't seen for a while. I crushed her in a long, quite public embrace—something I'd never before had the nerve to do. For the moment, I was a happy man. Had God accommodated my fear again?

Walter Allen Croom

8   Proving Grounds

Hitting that mile of tanks at the front door of Aberdeen's Proving Grounds rubbed in why I was there. But when I piled off the bus, the strong winds of the Chesapeake didn't exactly feel like Vietnam. And right now, I'd take winter a year if it helped me escape those jaws. Inside, First Sergeant was a kinder, gentler version of Sgt. Robinson.

"Boy, do you have a high school education?" was his first question. "No, I do not," I managed. "Well, can you type?" was the next one. "Just a little," I offered, wondering what my discover-and-land kind of Columbus typing had to do with my Fort Dix telecommunication training. But wouldn't you know that First Sergeant made me a clerk typist in the Officers' Field Ration Mess! That meant that every morning instead of rolling out to formations and tele- phone poles, I headed off to the military equivalent of a modern restaurant to type, keep the books, and col- lect officers' lunch money.

For the moment, I untensed—just a little bit. No KP or guard duty. No blood-and-guts drills. No vision of dangling from one of "Charlie's" poles. Only a uni- form. My fun was learning the native greetings of each current foreign officer—Iraqi, Libyan, Iranian, and Ethiopian—and then surprising each as he came through the chow line.

But that wasn't companionship. So the first Sunday after I arrived, I slipped into a Baptist church on the edge of the post. It felt good to be with Christians after five months of spiritual desert at Forts Bragg and Dix. But the next Sunday when two other guys and I headed off to take in the big town of Aberdeen, I stopped them at a brick-front building on North Philadelphia Boulevard. Its sign simply said, Aberdeen Servicemen's Christian Center. That looked good to me.

"Hey, fellows," I coaxed, "Let's go in and see what this place is." I could see they weren't terribly excited, but they followed me in. We had hardly shut the door when a graying friendly man stuck out his hand. "Welcome, I'm Earl Johnson, and this is the Aberdeen Christian Servicemen's Center."

"Walter Allen Croom," I offered gladly. The other fellows politely offered their names, but grudgingly followed as Rev. and Mrs. Johnson explained their way through the place's comfy-looking dining room, reading room, chapel, and dormitories. I couldn't believe such a place existed.

Outside again, it took me only one block down North Philadelphia Boulevard to decide I had to leave my friends and hustle back to take those kind Christians up on their offer. A soft bed, six home-cooked meals, and God's love every weekend—free. Man, did I need that kind of TLC. That started a comfortable routine. Every Friday, I hurried from post to my new home—and became one of Rev. and Mrs. Johnson's most eager "sons." I didn't realize until I found a father image like Rev. Johnson or cooking like Mrs. Johnson's that I was such a tight knot of overwork, fear and nervous habits.

Then six weeks after I had hugged her good-bye, Judy joined me, and we found a small cozy apartment above a pharmacy on Aberdeen's Main Street. It was nothing fancy, but we loved it. It was a place where we could be together. It let me get away from the things that made me churn with fear. And it was only a block from the Center where I had found spiritual help. I wanted to think that God had special-ordered such welcome Novocaine circumstances. But, I knew nothing so good could last for long—at least not if the Army had anything to do with it.

Lots of other fellows on post needed the same chance to shed their uniforms and meet God, so I jumped at the chance to give them the chance. Every Saturday evening about 6:00 p.m. a group of us "regulars" at the Servicemen's Center got together to pray, then work out a way to cover the whole post. We'd split into twos and hit every company, inviting every fellow we met to ride our bus over to the Center for an evening of good fun and fellowship.

Unless a fellow was a concrete agnostic, it wasn't hard to pry him loose from boredom. Even if he didn't especially feel like hearing about God, he rarely passed up the chance for a change. That's how it must have been with Ernie. One Saturday evening when one of us gave him an invitation card and explained what was for the taking, wild and woolly Ernie came along to give our tame place the once-around. He'd joined the Army to get away from a home without brothers and sisters. He certainly looked and acted the "tough" all right. He couldn't live without his bad habits, but looks were only the outside of his heart, and Ernie must have had a ready one. He listened very carefully that evening in the chapel service. Then he took up the speaker on his invitation and came to the front of the chapel asking for salvation. That evening Ernie was born again.

Only a blind and deaf person could have missed the change in Ernie. Once bored by us religious

63

"nuts," now he became a Center regular too. Friday evenings he'd sign up for a bunk and spend the whole weekend soaking up Scripture, canvassing the post with us, and telling the ones who came how special it was to know God. Months later, though, it still hadn't really occurred to Ernie that people might think it odd to see him slip them a Gospel tract with one hand and dangle a cigarette with the other. Ernie's past still dictated much of his life. But Ernie didn't like God's advice about such things and decided to ignore it. So he began skipping weekend visits. Then, he stopped coming altogether.

Several of us visited Ernie in his barracks, but he wasn't ready to admit that when a fellow stops going forward in his walk with God, there's only one other direction he can go. Several months later though, who stopped in at the Center one day but Ernie! This time, however, it wasn't for fellowship or counsel. This time it was to say good bye. He had gotten orders to the one place I just couldn't talk about.

I wasn't the one saying a possible forever good-bye, so I helped the others urge Ernie to take God with him. But when Ernie turned to me and said smartly, "Look, I've got only thirty days to live it up," I could see resentment all over him. What could I say? Thirty days and I'd probably still be counting lunch money. But Ernie was headed toward a Vietnam machine gun, and we both knew the survival rate for that job wasn't exactly anything to write home about.

A few months later, we heard from Ernie. He had sincerely made up with God, and he wanted to do the same with us. But it was as choking for me to listen to that letter as it was for Rev. Johnson to read it to us. Ernie's folks had received that letter with Ernie's body.

Why did fellows like Ernie have to sandpaper through my lunch-money security? It hurt. But why did I say security? I hadn't really ever known such a thing.

Judy's love had looked like security. And it was. But—wife or not—she hadn't been able to keep me out of the Army. And now with one after another of my Aberdeen friends shipping out, I knew counting officer's lunch money wouldn't keep me in the States. God was my only chance—again. But how much of a favored son was I?

I guess it was my prophecy professor at the Center's Bible Institute classes that kicked off my struggle to end another struggle. Dear old Howard Wheatly didn't even know he was filling that role. One evening in class, someone asked how secure a believer was in his salvation. I swallowed my breath at Prof. Wheatly's answer. I'd never met someone so adamant—or so wrong. He just stood up there in front of the class and insisted with all he could muster that a believer was as secure in God's eternal grasp of salvation as a finger was in a hand. After all, was that what God had meant in *John 10:28-30:*

> *And I give unto them eternal life, and*
> *they shall never perish, neither shall*
> *any man pluck them out of my hand.*
> *My father, who gave them to me, is*
> *greater than all, and no man is able to*
> *pluck them out of my Father's hand. I*
> *and my Father are one.*

No, I didn't think that's what it meant, I didn't think dear Pastor Johnson back in North Carolina thought so either. But I wouldn't say that to Prof. Wheatly, a fellow who wouldn't even sing a hymn with a theologically debatable word. So, I just took the battle home to my apartment. If I believed my salvation

65

was forever, wouldn't I get careless and commit some awful sin that might make God cancel my plans for heaven? Prof. Wheatly insisted John 6:37 answered that question with a big NO: "...he that cometh to me I will in no wise cast out."

It felt terrible to be in such a dilemma, so I turned to Aberdeen's Rev. Johnson. He had learned to read me like a father reads a son. In bits and pieces I dumped the problem. Strangely, Rev. Johnson agreed with Prof's. verses, but he also knew how to "shuck the matter right down to the cob" without upending me. He knew a verse for every objection, and an assurance for every fear. I seesawed back and forth— for months. Then slowly I came to the resolve that I must give up the fight, this time in God's favor. Maybe forever love was comfortable.

Initially, I found myself drifting away from the Lord. If forever meant forever, I no longer had to work as hard to keep myself in his grip. But slowly the truth of God's word began to penetrate my heart, and I realized that God loved me unconditionally. Something strange and wonderful began to happen in my life. I could identify with the Apostle Paul who said, "the love of Christ constrains me." Up to this point, I had been motivated by fear—fear that I would be rejected if I didn't live an orderly and obedient life. Now I realized, and for the first time began feeling, God holding onto me instead of me holding onto Him.

I had made the right decisions about relaxing. But doing that consistently was another matter. I had hugged fear to me for so long, I was afraid I'd feel unfinished without it. Judy's first miscarriage had cost me a hitch with the Army, and though I had to confess that I may have wanted that first child to shorten Vietnam's reach, at least now Judy and I both wanted a family for its own worth. I got to walk on clouds just a bit before Neil Armstrong of Apollo 11 got to walk on the moon. It was May 31, 1969, one of those Saturdays just made for picnics. Very pregnant Judy and I joined our Aberdeen Center sisters and brothers for an all-day picnic since Judy's three-week-away due date seemed safe enough to risk it. But when Mary Ann, one of the Center regulars, slipped up to me after the evening chapel service and whispered, "Judy needs the hospital now," I hurried her there afraid. Three weeks could make an important difference.

There was no use pacing the floors there at the hospital. No one would let me stay with Judy anyway. So back to the Center I went, not knowing how to fill the waiting. Bedtime came and went, and there was still no word. We had no phone in our apartment, so Rev. Johnson suggested I try bedding down in his office beside his phone. Finally at 5:45 a.m. Sunday morning, I got the call that I was the father of a baby boy weighing a nice 5 lb. 14 oz. Since that sounded secure enough, you can be sure I shared the particulars with every half-interested fellow that joined us for that Sunday morning Bible study. But then in the middle of a hymn, a note came my way. I unrolled it to read, "Call the doctor at the hospital."

"Oh, God, now what?" I moaned all the way to the phone. "Young man," came the doctor's tired but professional voice. "Your baby is experiencing severe respiratory difficulties. His survival depends on special care at Walter Reed Army Medical Center in Washington. We'll go by ambulance."

I climbed into that dull Army ambulance and looked at Timothy Paul in his incubator. I'd waited for him for what seemed like forever. Now I couldn't do anything about his tiny chest flapping like a sail in a bay storm. Judy and I really wanted him. I was sure I wanted him more for Judy than for me. I wanted to be a father, but Judy needed to be a mother.

The whole thing scared me out of my wits. But this time, I told myself, I was not going to let it scare me out of my faith. I'd do what dear Prof. Wheatly had just been urging us students to do—talk to God like He knew what He was doing.

"God," I whispered, "Would you let this little one stay with us? I don't know how; that's Your business. But we'd sure appreciate it." I looked at my watch. About 11:30 a.m. Rev. Johnson had probably just finished the morning worship service hymns. I bent over to see Timothy Paul again. His chest was still hammering. But, say...my heart wasn't. It had resumed its normal pace. And, I felt good, real good. In fact, I felt...maybe that was what you called peace.

The rest of the way to Washington blurred past the ambulance. I sat there watching. At Walter Reed, a nice white-vested doctor decided Timothy Paul's chances were 50-50. A nice even chance for either fear or hope. But neither gripped me. Just the somehow hard-to-explain feeling that this time I could relax because God knew more about such things than I did.

Back at Aberdeen, I wasn't really too surprised to find out that Rev. Johnson had stopped the morning worship service to pray for healing for Timothy Paul and peace for Judy and me. But what surprised me was the time. He had done it about 11:30 a.m., just when I was talking to God. Timothy Paul made it. I did too.

About the time Timothy Paul was able to sit up alone, Rev. Johnson suggested Judy and I move into the apartment above the Center so I could share in the ministry. Sensing God's approval, we made the move. The place was rent-free and a chance to really serve. But, why do I say really serve? I was already studying at the Center's Bible Institute Monday evening, canvassing the barracks Tuesday evening, attending post chapel service Wednesday evening, joining Center personnel for a Thursday evening meeting, and welcoming fellows to the Center Friday, Saturday and Sunday. Maybe I should say I was just parked closer to my over-involvement. At least that's how Mary Ann had sized it up.

There was perhaps no more bubbly and thoughtful person around the Center than Mary Ann. Yet she had returned a simple, "Walt, you're not indispensable," several months before when I had reminded Judy and her how important it was that I help Rev. Johnson all I could. Honestly, I didn't think either God or Rev. Johnson were in trouble if he didn't have my help. And I knew Mary Ann never spoke to hurt. So was I needing to be needed more than wanting to help? Maybe. Then Rev. Johnson tilted my world a little more. He had decided to move to Baltimore to pastor a church. That meant he wouldn't be there at the center handy for me...Monday, Tuesday, Wednesday...

But what good did it do to pout? Rev. Johnson's successor, Rev. J. Frank Lilley was a tonic. Serious and silly, enthusiastic and realistic, he picked me up—fear and all—right where Rev. Johnson had gently set me down. Then he wondered out loud whether or not Judy and I would be willing to stay at the Center until May. Why May? Oh, sure. That was when I would get to chuck my uniform—that uniform that had split me wide open with fear. Sure, I'd stay until May. Really, I wanted to stay a lot longer than that. Certainly not so I could wear that uniform and worry about Vietnam, but just so I could stay close to the Center and its spiritual Geritol.

Rev. Lilley thought that it might be better for us to stay on longer than May and commute to a nearby Bible school than to pack our bags and wander off to Bible school in South Carolina. But before I could enroll in Bible school, I had some unfinished business that needed to be taken care of. I needed affirmation of that GED that the draft had interrupted. So Judy, young Timothy Paul, and I jumped into our car and hurried back down to North Carolina and my GED records. To claim that GED, I needed a raw score of 225. The teacher I needed to get that score from said I had a 224½. 1 was speechless, so I just inwardly turned my mind to Philippians 4:13 and waited.

"Well, I may round that 224½ either up or down. So, son, I'll round that up." smiled Mr. Henderson, who had also been my 8th grade shop teacher, and was as proud of handing me my diploma as I was of receiving it.

With that provision, I was off to Lancaster School of the Bible. Every morning Jim Cordell and I rolled out of the sack and hit the road about 5:30 a.m. Each week we alternated. One of us drove while the other snatched a few more minutes of dozing. Just before we crossed the state line into Pennsylvania, we would pull into a small restaurant and get a cup of coffee and doughnut. Then it was back to the road and college. Usually we pulled into the college parking lot and madly dashed toward class. After classes were over for the day, we headed back to Aberdeen, sometimes at a more leisurely pace. As a native of the lowlands of North Carolina, I sometimes asked Jim to stop so I could take pictures of the beautiful rolling hills and lovely farms of Lancaster County. I was fascinated when we were slowed down by Amish horses and buggies. A little like mail-carriers, Jim and I made our appointed rounds through rain, sleet or snow—for one whole school year.

Saturday night chapel program at the Military
Christian Center in Aberdeen.

Dedication of our
multi-purpose building in 1987.

9   Failing at Success

That first year at Lancaster School of the Bible I obsessed on over-achievement. Larry, the male half of a young couple raising financial support so they could go to Iceland as missionaries, so passed on his excitement for serving the Lord that I took up his challenge to memorize the book of Romans. But to do that, I had to conveniently "forget" that I was a full-time student at Lancaster School of the Bible, that I was attending Monday evening laymen's classes at the Maryland Bible Institute, that I was helping out at Aberdeen's Servicemen's Christian Center, and that I was a husband and a father.

I shouldn't have been surprised that, though I managed to make it through the first year of school, it was only two weeks into the summer that I received an official letter from the academic dean informing me that my poor grades would not allow me to return. I thought I would die. There was nothing more I wanted in life than to go to school. That had been all I had dreamed about for the last several years. I had no idea what I would tell my dear mother and my poor wife. So I called the school and made an appointment to see Dean Figart. He must have sensed my intensity because he graciously consented to my plea for just one more chance. I had to make some adjustments. Like Richard Nixon, then president, I diplomatically informed Rev. Frank Lilley, the director of the Aberdeen Serviceman's Christian Center, that my family and I would be moving our residence closer to my chosen campus of study. Accordingly, we relocated in a quaint, tree-sheltered little house just off Hartman Station Road near the small Lancaster County, PA town of Leola.

Perhaps the only thing that did for me, however, was to help me intensify my distractions. My daily schedule was grueling: school from 7 a.m. to 2:30 p.m., work from 3:30-10 p.m., study until the early hours of the morning, then a few hours I excused as "rest," and back to the classroom at 7 a.m. Saturday, it was bus visitation. Sunday, I taught a Sunday School class. On top of all that, anytime Pastor Lilley suggested he could use a little extra help, I hurried back to Aberdeen and the Serviceman's Christian Center.

That certainly wasn't the wisest way for me to live. Studying was not the easiest task for me anyway, and now I was taking things like Greek, homiletics, and hermeneutics. No wonder I feared I might end up disappointing Dr. Figart by failing a second time.

Added to the growing list of things I was feebly shouldering were what might be euphemistically termed "cash flow problems." I was ever so grateful that my two years of military service had qualified me for GI financing of my studies—I would not have been able to afford it otherwise—but I still had to keep bread on the table. That I considered my responsibility, because our son Paul was still a toddler and needed his mother home with him.

Of course, that made things tight. Many winter evenings we slept next to the open oven door because we had no fuel to heat our quaint little house. And even though we could manage fuel for the car, the old vehicle decided to quit. The mechanic at the neighborhood garage just looked at me when I grumbled, "I feel like Job."

"What in the world happened?" he asked.

"Did you lose your children?"

"No, sir," I admitted.

"Well, did you lose your good health?"

"No, sir."

"Well, then," he corrected, "You're no Job."

He was right and I had been rebuked.

But I was still feeling pretty low when I went to pick up a replacement car someone had offered us in return for paying its small repair bill.

"Oh, by the way," the repairman explained when I picked up the car, "Sometimes it won't start when you turn over the ignition key. You might have to try this." He lifted the hood and touched something with a screwdriver. I watched what he did.

You would have thought that he would have repaired that problem too, but he hadn't, so I figured it would do no good for me to complain. Really, I didn't want to complain because I was just ever so glad not to have to walk everywhere. So I just paid the bill, got into the car, and confirmed that mechanic's suggestion that the car wouldn't start. Out came a screwdriver, up went the hood, and down the road I went in our "new" 1960 green Impala Chevrolet.

Of course, when I came back out from a very short stop at the grocery store, that old clunker wouldn't start again. So out came the screwdriver again. I made it home, got a quick bite to eat, changed my clothes, kissed Judy good-bye, and headed back to the car to go to my evening employment. It wouldn't start. But now I was an expert. The next thing I found myself doing, however, was literally catapulting myself a good distance away from that car so I wouldn't get run over by my own car. No one had ever told me that if I "under-the-hood" started an automatic when it was in drive, it would take off.

I tried running alongside, hoping I could reach the door handle, yank it open, and jump in. That I finally managed to do, but before I could hit the brake, that obstreperous car of mine had allowed a telephone pole at the edge of our property to knock out a headlamp, damage the hood, and poke a hole in the radiator.

That was about as elastic as my emotions were just then, so I picked up a convenient board and smashed it across the side of that offending car. "God," I mumbled, "Why are you doing this to me? I give you my life for the ministry and this is what I get in return?"

Judy stepped out onto our back porch. She had heard. "Walt, you've trusted God before," she soothed. "He's never let you down. Trust Him again."

I knew Judy was right. God proved just as generous as things were tight or inconvenient. One evening at work, a former student approached me and slipped me $30.00. I wondered how he knew about such little secrets as our eating only eggs for three days in a row. We didn't have a phone so my wife could not have told his wife, and I certainly never told anyone our needs. When I asked, he smiled knowingly. "Well, Walter," he said, "I, too, was once a student."

But I still worried...and acted in haste. Lines at the gas station were getting longer because prices were skyrocketing. I guess Arab nations figured that if they stopped shipping oil, they could "get U.S. back" for helping Israel in the Yom Kippur War. I wasn't sure of all that implied or involved, but even my pastor, a bold, fiery man, turned his sermons into strong suggestions that we transfer our currency into silver so we wouldn't run the risk of becoming "worse than an infidel" when things got so bad we could no longer "provide for our own."

Those ideas made even more sense to me when I read the little book our pastor began offering to everyone in our congregation. There I read that during hard times, only gold and silver would retain value.

"Perhaps they're right," I fussed. "I certainly don't want my family to end up in real financial trouble. I'll be responsible. I better act."

Though I could hardly keep food on the table, I hurried to the local bank and borrowed six hundred dollars. Before I hurried off to the local coin shop to purchase an equal amount of silver coins, the loan officer set me up for one year of monthly repayments.

Before long, however, I had more to worry about than silver coins I had hidden. First, the carburetor of that good old green Chevrolet developed problems. It's repair job did not hold, and we ended up buying a new one anyway. Then while we were visiting our family in North Carolina over Christmas, the clutch needed to be replaced. Back home in PA after the holidays, the clutch "kicked up" again. Apparently that North Carolina mechanic had improperly installed the first clutch, and it had burned out. That meant another clutch, but it was at our expense.

It hurt...deeply...but I was forced to keep cashing in a few more of those stashed coins. Within two months I had no coins and ten more months of bank payments. By the end of 1974, nothing had crashed and I had to admit that it was "better to trust in the Lord than to put confidence in man" (Ps. 118:8).

I could mentally acknowledge God's goodness and greater wisdom, but I had yet to find daily peace. Sometimes I felt so pressured, that I literally bent over gasping. Only a few weeks away from my B.S. degree in Biblical Studies, I could easily explain how to find the peace of God that "passes all understanding." But I had yet to regularly experience that peace.

10 Freer to Serve

May 17th was a special day. That day I mounted the platform of the school's gymnasium, walked resolutely toward Dr. Stuart Lease, President of Lancaster Bible College, firmly shook his hand, and walked away tightly clutching a diploma.

I had made it the whole way through.

I...my family...my mother...all shared that proud- and humbling-moment. For the moment "I can do all things through Christ who strengthens me" (Philippians 4:13) crowded out my eternal companion—dread of rejection, fear of failure.

As a freshman I had determined to become an evangelist. Now, after graduating, I had my heart set on the pastorate. There was only one little problem, I had no church. So to keep us in food until I found that church, I began scouring the classified section of the local newspaper. There were these two possibilities: working at a Woolworth distribution center or coordinating a group of 23 developmentally challenged young adults employed by Goodwill Industries. Both accepted my application.

The pay at Woolworth's was good, and the job site was close enough for me to walk. The Goodwill job would mean a thirty-minute drive to the nearby city of Lancaster. But I decided that such considerations were of little consequence since either job, as I figured, would be only temporary. God had called me into the pastorate. I decided to choose between the two with a simple question: In which job can I best apply my Bible training?

Working with the young adults at Goodwill Industries seemed the best answer, but I had no formal training in working effectively with the developmentally challenged. Yet, I chose that over the Woolworth offer because there I figured I could put to use at least some of my Bible School training. The longer ride to work and the reduced income seemed less important than the possible chance to make some spiritual contribution to another person's life.

I took literally what the Bible said about good working relationships, so I made a few operating adjustments. If the developmentally challenged workers performed well, I rewarded them. If they did not, I withheld such privileges as leaving their workstations during break. Each afternoon, I took just enough time to hold character guidance classes in which they could learn to manage emotions such as anger. Weekly, I conducted the chapel service Goodwill held for its employees. The input brought good output. Some developed less offensive hygiene habits. Others became kinder, at times even forgiving, toward co-workers. Most developed acceptable work habits. I most remember the change in Selma, a middle-aged woman with the mentality of a five-year old. Other supervisors told me she had known such little self-control that she had once, in an outburst of anger, plunged a pair of scissors into another worker. Now, as she slowly began to recognize anger building up, she substituted the better habit of throwing up her hands, hurrying for the door, and screaming out her frustrations.

Soon, where there had been disorganization and rowdiness, there was now structure, organization and tranquillity. Heads of other departments commented on the great job I was doing, and I accepted the affirmation as a confirmation that I was where God wanted me—for just a little while.

Yet, each day when I got back home and settled down on the couch to relax, depression turned me into a modern Atlas. I, too, carried the world on my shoulders. I even stooped to snapping at Judy and our young son, Timothy Paul.

Sure, this was where I was supposed to be right then. But anybody could do that job. I was to be the pastor of a church, and that place was certainly not a church.

Several months later, Ben Weaver suggested that I join him in developing a rehab program to help emotionally maladjusted persons as they transitioned from institutional care back into the community. What he envisioned was a "halfway house" with a program that stressed Biblical living principles. My job would be to reproduce the same transformations in his center as I had seen happen in my department. Ben wanted the Center to direct its services specifically toward those that were emotionally maladjusted. It would be a halfway house between a mental services institution and the community. I suppose Ben figured that if there had been such a transformation in my program at Goodwill, I could engineer the same thing at the center he desired to establish. The several times Ben approached me about linking up to start a new work, I declined, politely reminding him that I wanted to pastor a church. I was simply in a holding pattern until God opened the door. But when God held the door open for me, I didn't get to walk into a church. I got to walk out of Goodwill. A simple management upheaval, and I was out of a job. I picked up the phone and called Ben.

"Do you still need someone for that center of yours?" I asked.

"Yes, Walt, I do," he said assuredly.

"Okay, I'll be your Director of Rehabilitation," I said. "But, remember, I'll be moving on to a pastorate."

In the meantime, though, there was lots of work to do. From November of 1975 until January of 1976, when Ben and I opened the doors of the Lighthouse Rehabilitation Center near the town of New Holland, PA, we worked to the tune of hammer and saw, bringing an old fire-station building up to state code so that we could mingle personal client work projects with individualized counseling.

That first month of operations, we assisted just two clients. However, within eighteen months we had four full-time workers, two part-time workers and a building full of clients. It was wonderful to see God birthing people into His family, and just as thrilling to see others' lives turn quite around. Marie had medically "anti-depressed" herself in and out of institutions for several years. Lucy needed all kinds of spiritual "revamping." Peggy had punctuated her years of missionary work with several periods of hospitalization because runaway worry had induced severe insomnia, chemical imbalance and a temporary inability to perceive reality correctly.

John, however, had never lost his grip on reality. He had just figured that pretending he had might get him his own way. For example, if he rolled his eyes out of alignment, I was supposed to pity him and give him "early leave" to visit home. One day I stopped him in the middle of his antics and said quite frankly,

"John, stop that irresponsible behavior."

John just looked at me. Then we had a good conversation.

All clients had unique problems. Special backgrounds and different faulty ways of attempting to "work things out." Yet all responded and improved only as they—through continual and continued counseling—discovered how to integrate God's Word into their minds and lives. Marie needed peace more than medicine. Lucy responded to spiritual cleansing. Peggy realized that in order to break her downward spiral, she had to focus on faith living. John slowly accepted the disciplines of godliness.

Blonde, twenty year-old Anna Marie appeared to be one person who might not need our services very long. She seemed to progress quickly and smoothly. Then one day, when we took our usual break from work projects to pray and talk, Anna Marie casually mentioned that she had visited a fortuneteller, and things turned a sharp corner.

I didn't know whether Anna Marie had seen *The Exorcist, Rosemary's Baby,* or *Children of the Corn*—all occult films that had hit the box office. But I was curious. I had read just enough of Merrill Unger's Christian perspective and at Lancaster Bible College had heard German Professor Kurt Koch lecture on demon activity, so I probed for details about her visit with the fortuneteller. Anna Marie switched topics. I played along but slowly worked my conversational way back to the offending matter. The next time I brought it up, she did the same thing. Then, suddenly, and without apparent cause, she appeared to have been pushed off her chair. There she lay on the floor unconscious, but her body lay in exactly the same position she had been sitting in.

A co-worker almost immediately opened the door to investigate the strange commotion she had overheard. Both of us stood there blankly. Slowly, I knelt down, patted Anna Marie on the cheek. She woke up, looked around, and asked what had happened.

I knew very little about demons, but I knew I had seen into just a few fringe shadows of deep spiritual darkness. After my co-worker and I lifted Anna Marie to her knees, I spoke quite directly. "Anna Marie, I want to talk to you. All I want you to do is listen."

I began speaking, "Unclean spirit, I command you to come out of Anna Marie." Anna Marie again fell to the floor. She shook. She foamed at the mouth.

"Demons, name yourselves," I continued,

One by one I heard names. Each voice sounded like Anna Marie's. Each voice had a strong bass over-lay. Each voice sounded as though it came from far below Anna Marie's larynx.

"You may have kicked me out of heaven," one voice commented, "but you're not going to kick me out of here."

Another demon added a comment. Then another. But no demon would relinquish its hold on Anna Marie, I had heard that demons fear mention of Christ's blood, so both my co-worker and I decided to invoke the power of Christ's shed blood. When we did, Anna Marie's arms and legs began to swing wildly. Not knowing what else to do, I ran into the workroom and asked all who were true believers in Christ to stop working and begin pray-ing for Anna Marie. Then I hurried back to Anna Marie.

"In the power of Christ's blood, come out of her, you evil spirits," I commanded. Nothing. Not even voices. I prayed again. Nothing. Again. Nothing.

"Anna Marie, would you be willing to receive Christ as your personal Savior?" I asked ever so gently.

"Yes," she slowly responded, but with ease.

I knew that God was honoring the prayers of our godly staff. Together we helped Anna Marie quietly turn her heart and body over to God. The next day when my co-worker said something to Anna Marie about her release, she came running to my office.

"Did those awful things really happen to me?" she begged, frantic with fear.

"Whatever was true yesterday, Anna Marie, is not true today," I assured. "Jesus now lives in your heart and life."

From then on there was nothing. God had granted her a total memory lapse on that particular matter. Her mind bore no scars of her bondage to Satan. The whole thing reminded me of the man from Gadara out of whom Jesus had cast demons. He too was "in his right mind" when the townspeople came out to see what had happened.

Another co-worker, however, questioned, "Walt, was Anna Maria pretending?"

"If she was," I assured him, "it was the best acting I have ever seen."

Why I had been permitted to momentarily glimpse into the demonic abuse enveloping Anna Marie, I could not say. I knew I had no intentions of stirring around in such darkness. True, Anna Marie had been the unusual client, but I was also encountering plenty of others with less than normal behavior. Sometimes their behavior was easily traced back to the abuse of a drug—legal or illegal. More often than not, however, their acting out proved to be either the complaint of a dysfunctioning body or the attempts of a violated conscience to rid itself of guilt.

I knew the answers to such problems. Fix the medical problem or confess the guilt. But what I didn't know how to deal with—at the moment—was my own emerging pattern of depression. Here, behind my desk at The Lighthouse Rehabilitation Center I could help others move toward inner peace. But that was the only place.

Every morning I had to will myself out of bed. It was a struggle to push my feet toward the bathroom. When I finally made it to the kitchen, food made me nauseated. Driving to work, I forced myself to sing so that I would be in some decent frame of mind when I got there. But once there, behind that desk or zipping through my daily routine, things brightened up and life looked good—until I called it a day. I needed to understand more about my own problems.

In the Scriptures I found such "greats" as King David and Elijah struggling. Commenting on his own waywardness, King David mused, "Why are you cast down, O my soul? And why are you disquieted within me?" And that great prophet Elijah—after a stunning victory on Mount Carmel—hit emotional bottom so hard that he had even asked God to take his life.

With a whole lot more reading, I came to the conclusion that though psychologists were stressing "mental" or "psychological" distress as a major root cause of what I knew was professionally termed "depression," Scripture appeared to highlight only the "organic" and "spiritual." I had no reason to believe that my depression was physical. I wasn't experiencing highs and lows and exaggerated mood swings. I had none of the symptoms of the kind of bipolar condition that responds to lithium carbonate. I simply felt as though I were responsible to bear the burdens of the whole world on my shoulders.

About the only possibility I was left with was that my problems were spiritual. Yet, how could this be? I faithfully led my family to church. I was having both family and personal devotions. I was memorizing Scripture. I was witnessing. I had a B.S. degree in

Bible. I didn't lie or steal. I always went the second or third mile for others.

Slowly, a deep conviction settled on me that what was wrong was that I had developed a mental disposition that was in direct opposition to Scripture. I had developed some faulty thinking patterns. Since thinking was what was affecting my acting, I could expect depression as long as I operated on faulty thoughts.

The Apostle Paul and other authors of Scripture had not neatly packaged all the verses that addressed right thinking under a single heading, but with the help of a Bible concordance, I carefully ferreted out five simple steps I could take:

(1) Discard faulty thinking patterns
     (II Corinthians 10:5)
(2) Renew my thinking processes
     (Romans 12:2; Ephesians 4:23)
(3) Think wholesome, godly thoughts
     (Philippians 4:8)
(4) Combine believing what God said,
     with doing what God said (James 2:18)
(5) Allow the Holy Spirit to empower
     my mind and life (Galatians 5:22-26)

Obviously, I was responsible for my emotional state. Taking responsibility would mean more than just memorizing Scripture, but those steps seemed far less complicated than Sigmund Freud's kind of psychotherapy—and a whole lot less time-consuming and expensive. I could keep on blaming my father—who indeed had contributed to my dis-ease—or I could step up to the home base of personal responsibility and swing away at the problem.

It looked easier and a whole lot more promising to choose the latter. So, what had been wrong with my thinking? That took thought, but in time I handed myself three indictments:

(1) I was discontent
(2) I was unthankful
(3) I was negative

Such self-accusations felt a bit harsh, but I knew they were true. All the while I was introducing clients to peace despite handicaps, I was also staring beyond the luscious grass of Lighthouse service to the envied "greener" pastures of pastoring a church. I had also forgotten that God had held my hand the whole way from life along a dirt road in North Carolina through Bible College. I had hardly been appreciative for that kind of grace, love and mercy. And I was negative. Life—even the chance to serve there at the Lighthouse—was a glass I called half-empty rather than half-full.

The long and short of it all was that I had a poor definition of success. God was sovereign; He was in control of even the "bad" things I had and would keep on experiencing. So why, if He would make everything work "together" for His purposes, why was I full of worry and fear? Of course, I didn't want to fail. Nor did I want someone to reject me. But working feverishly, often to near exhaustion, just to prevent either from happening was silly. I had to admit my strange definition of "success" would not bring significance.

My goal was set. As I began to think right thoughts about who God is and where I fit into His kingdom, a major miracle unfolded in my life. As I began to think God's thoughts after Him, I began to act right. And as I began to act in accordance with Scriptural principles, I actually began to feel right.

A winter afternoon in 1977, as I was about to leave the Lighthouse, weather newscasts were warning of a severe blizzard. I knew it would be wise to head right home, but I also knew that I needed to stop for some groceries. It was scary to walk those aisles and hear everyone commenting about how violent the wind was becoming and how driven the snow was, so I headed to the window to see for myself. They were right. The wind was howling at a tremendous rate and blowing snow, pebbles and practically everything in its path.

My heart began to palpitate. My mind shouted. *Leave, Walt; get out of here.* I began scrambling through one aisle after another almost blindly grabbing things. Suddenly there was God's promise to be with me, to never leave me. It was a struggle. That sounded good. But my heart was palpitating and my legs ached to run.

Stop! I ordered myself. I came to a halt—taking one step and then another.

I will never leave...never forsake...

I actually strolled through the store until my cart was filled. It was so satisfying.

That was the very first time I had controlled fear by controlling my thoughts.

But it was not to be the last. The next thing I targeted—and saw slowly dissipate—were those obsessive-compulsive behaviors I had so long hugged to myself as an emotional security blanket. Finally, I no longer needed to scratch my right hand if I scratched my left. Gone were the second and third trips out of bed to check already locked doors. I simply refused to act on the impulses I knew by now Satan was using to bind me. *You can no longer force me to do things that are not Scriptural. My authority is Scripture. I will listen only to it.*

I had submitted to radical surgery. Now it was time to heal. But healing from hurt is one thing, and helping others heal was another. Studying the best way to make the second happen while I myself was busy with the first was an almost over-ambitious task. Yet that was exactly the course I pursued. While I counseled others at the Lighthouse Rehabilitation Center—and battled my own depression—I studied counseling at a training facility in Philadelphia, PA.

It was an exciting over-commitment, though. What I heard in the classroom I soon learned to spot, both in my own actions and reactions, then in the lives of those I counseled at the Rehabilitation Center. It was easy to identify, to empathize. I had been there, done that. I knew the feeling. I knew the struggle.

One thing soon became clear. I was not going to find myself in the pastorate, at least not in a local church. That may have been my dream for ever so long, but now the Lord was making it clear that that was not what He had planned for me. I was better equipped to counsel others. I was comfortable. So were my counselees. I operated with ease. My counselees responded positively. I knew just what I would do. I would hang out my own counseling shingle. For now though, I would solo counsel after hours. I needed to earn while I learned. If I counseled by day for the Rehabilitation Center, I could counsel by night on my own. Then when I had finally finished my counseling studies, I could transition to a solo practice. Things would prove easier—and more practical—that way.

Soon, however, easy and practical no longer seemed the most important points of consideration. I felt myself being pulled in the direction of starting a counseling center right then. I heard no voices, saw nothing in the sky. I just believed God was speaking directly to my spirit. God's direction or not, however, I immediately knew fear. My family. Judy's family. My mother. What would they think if I walked away from the stable job I had at the Rehabilitation Center? Money? The little bit of moonlight counseling I was doing would hardly cover food on the table. I'd still have rent, phone, gas, electric...*Lord, just how would I do all that?*

But none of the reasonable rationalizing I did seemed to lessen the pull I felt toward just such a move. I became restless. I began to significantly differ with just enough of minor policy matters around the Center that I had to finally admit that my continued presence would create increasing disharmony. So, in time, I submitted my resignation.

But—like me—I just couldn't make myself head off to that solo counseling center I had planned on. Instead I found myself another job—working on an assembly line in the city of Lancaster. There I stood for ten hours a day, in one position, assembling hair dryers and beauty products as they marched meaninglessly before me on the conveyer belt.

Soon, I was plagued by a sickening head cold I could not shake. I was also as uncomfortable as Jonah. I guess Jonah knew more than he cared to know about the Ninevites he was supposed to "counsel." Offend them and they might just carve you up with glass shards and hang you on a pole outside the city—as an example. Afraid that the kind of "example" God wanted him to be to the Ninevites might just turn him into the kind they hung outside their city wall, he had headed in the opposite direction.

Of course, I didn't think I was the same kind of disobedient coward as Jonah had been, so I broached the subject with my pastor when, one day I had to ask him to rescue me from a car so overheated that I had to abandon it on my way to work. We had quite a long conversation on the way to his office. There, as we talked our way through the "faith" steps of Hebrews 11, I realized I needed to put my full weight on God's promises. I would have to believe what that great missionary Hudson Taylor had observed: Where God's finger points, His hand will provide.

After a while, both of us got down on our knees. With my pastor's encouragement that sometimes the only thing that makes sense is obeying, I offered God my fear and committed to doing what I perceived to be His immediate will for me.

We stood up. Gone was the apprehension, the fear, that had nagged me for months. The next day at work, I handed in my two-week notice. Surprisingly— or perhaps not so surprising—was the fact that with that move, that nasty cold also vanished.

11 Serving to Free

If all it takes to make a school—as Mark Twain once commented—is a log with a teacher on one end and a student on the other, then I guess all I really needed for a counseling center were two chairs and one counselee.

Really, that was about all I had; a couple of chairs, but no place to put them. It was almost unnerving to act on faith. I felt as though I first needed to finish my training, to establish a financial base. It seemed I was being pushed into the obedience I so much wanted to be choosing. Maybe what it was that unnerved me, however, was something even I could sense but not verbalize—a lingering fear that my Heavenly Father might operate like my flesh-and-blood father.

I didn't have long to fret. A local business man, Wesley Burkholder, took care of a place for chairs. Next to a busy highway, in one of three mobile home parks he owned, sat an empty 8' x 40' mobile unit he had long before used as a sales office. Though it now had no electricity or water and needed lots of repair, the unit was a quite satisfactory starter office. I found an old-fashioned kerosene heater—the kind that dared you to turn your back. Friend Bill Hoffman helped me rig up a gaslight that may have sputtered but shed light on things. Somewhere I managed a desk. March 1978, I opened the only front door there was!

The graciousness of everyone involved in that new venture was quite a boost for my tentative faith.

93

Clients' cars became waiting rooms. With no running water—and therefore, no restrooms—one client graciously excused herself, took advantage of the facilities of the nearby bowling lane, and returned to pick up our interrupted conversation as unruffled as if we had paused for a mutual sneeze! Occasionally, I needed to practice the same nonchalance. Once when I hurried to the local burger establishment between counselees, I returned to find my kerosene challenge had spewed all kinds of soot across those chairs and that desk. I just got busy wiping!

A part-time secretary, Joan Patterson, was the thoughtful contribution of my church. Each morning about 9:00 a.m. Joan arrived to begin taking phone calls, scheduling afternoon and evening consultations, and doing the hundred little things that run an office. By then I had spent devotional time alone with the Lord and was ready to begin my day. Knowing that until I developed a clientele, I would have plenty of hours to occupy, I decided to spend some of them learning. I had enrolled in an external degree study program, so each morning I studied intensely, then during the afternoon and evening counseled whatever counselees were scheduled.

Before I submitted my lessons for credit, Joan graciously typed them. She occasionally teased that she should get part of my projected degree for typing all those lessons. When she finally did add college to her already busy life of raising two small children, she credited her desire to study to those hours she had spent making sense of my handwriting.

Another way I filled the opportunities between counseling sessions was to introduce others to this new ministry in any way I could. I couldn't afford a regular radio program, so I came up with one-minute segments I called "Tips for Living." I wrote carefully scripted material and found I could pack an amazing amount of information into one minute of air time. In this way a number of people came to the center because they had been first attracted to the practical advice of those quick minutes.

Longer air time came as the Blue Ridge Cable Network of Ephrata, PA offered me air time after one of their game shows. Friends supplied the financial means, and for about a year, I counseled teens over the airwaves. In addition, any time I planned a seminar, scheduled an open house or proposed a new project, I sent the information to both that and other local radio stations. Both they and the local newspapers were quite willing to offer free coverage because the center was set up as a not-for-profit organization.

By 1979, when our third child, Jonathan, was born, I had moved to larger quarters and added an Institute of Christian Counseling that twice a year trained students in counseling techniques. In 1981 the Institute expanded into an external home study program, which today allows students from both the United States and overseas to study Biblical principles of Christian counseling in their own homes.

Though my first wobbly steps of faith may have been somewhat motivated by desperation, it dawned on me that my operational definitions were slowly changing. Unlike Vince Lombardi, I no longer felt that "winning" was the only thing that mattered. It was far less vital for me to attain "position," be "happy," or feel "approved." I was beginning to experience a little bit of each, but no longer were they vital to my "success." That was now becoming something I could much more easily trade for surrender.

But I had to admit that trust was still a challenge. I possessed salvation. That was unquestionable. I had

God's approval. That was becoming much more comfortable. I had God's promises. And he had kept those before. There had been soup when that was what my family needed. A car when that was what I needed. A pair of shoes. Whatever. But this time I had bills. Big ones. And I had no intentions of defaulting. But intentions wouldn't pay bills. So one Saturday morning, I paced and whined—just a little.

"God, you took me this far. But now I feel abandoned. You know...those bills..."

Somebody's knocking on the door interrupted my complaining. It was Wesley.

"Walter," he said slipping a check into my hand, "I have been meaning to give you this for sometime, but it simply slipped my mind."

Later, a husband and wife stopped by to give me a little plastic sandwich bag. They said it was their way of saying thanks for helping restore their marriage. When I looked, that little bag held something not so little. It contained a rather large sum of money.

So, how long could I whimper in distrust? I guess I just didn't like that feeling of impending disaster as I blindly teetered on the brink of what always proved to be God's bottomless and measureless supplies.

For some reason, the Lord repeatedly sent counselees who—like me—were seeking release from the consequences of fear. Marge was unhappy because she had allowed fear of academic failure to keep her from the college education she desired. John had lost the respect of his wife, the obedience of his children, and the cooperation of his co-workers because he feared decisiveness. Fearing the loneliness of life without the husband who had left her, Martha had twice toyed with suicide. Janelle felt so overwhelmed by caring for the children her husband's accidental death had left in her care that she feared she might physically harm them.

I could point no finger. I had waked the same route. I was stiff succumbing at times. But I was learning, like David of old, that I could indeed "lay down in peace and sleep; for thou Lord, only [made] me dwell in safety." So as we together looked at the Word and together found the principles He had intended as antidotes for each life-sized fear, we both found increasing liberation. Behind the desk at the counseling center, I may have appeared the teacher, but I too was learning under the Greater Teacher. My classroom was the classroom of service. Both I and those I shared with were learning to walk by faith.

Of course, even that faith met it's test. Mine came in the form of a phone call.

"Son, Granddad has died," Mom's familiar voice drawled as her call interrupted my nightly ritual of watching the 6 o'clock evening news. I heard the familiar mix of emotion and matter-of-fact statement.

The news was hardly unexpected. Granddad had been born way back in 1887, so by now—March 29, 1981—he had already passed 93 milestones of life. His had been a long life on the farm. I had certainly profited. My fourteen-year-old ache for companionship was certainly benefitted by Granddad's willingness to let me work on his farm and tag along to tobacco markets. But now not only were those privileges a memory; so was Granddad's life.

"And," continued Moms' quiet voice, "when the family cleaned out Granddad's house, they found a letter tucked between the mattress halves of his bed."

"Walter Allen, that letter was from your dad."

Silence. For a long moment. I knew Dad had neither learned to read nor write, so obviously someone had written it for him. It bore a Washington, D.C. address.

"Son, I think your dad should be notified," Mother continued.

That was so like my dear mother-thinking of the needs of a husband and father who had years before quite literally vanished. But, yes, I too felt that Dad should be notified of his father's death.

"Mom, Judy and I will meet you tomorrow in Washington," I promised.

I had been there, done that...before. Several years before after an especially disturbing dream, a friend, Cormie Hildebrand, and I had scoured a Washington D.C. bus station where a North Carolina friend thought he had seen Dad, but the search had proved fruitless.

But I had so long dreamed—sometimes to the point of nightmares—of finding Dad. I would try again. That next day in the Capitol parking lot, after the little huddle of Crooms had swelled to include my mother, my sister, three of my four brothers, and I, we all hurried off to find what we assumed the address on Dad's letter suggested as an apartment building.

We found the street, but no apartment building. That had long since been razed. The next logical place to head seemed to be the old paint company for whom Dad had worked so many years before. But, again, at that location there was no longer any such company.

Finding Dad just didn't look too promising. Maybe it would prove impossible. After all, that letter was dated 1974 and a lot happens during a period of seven years. A subdued bunch of Crooms, we decided to spend the night at my Pennsylvania home and resume our search the following day. I, however, would not be able to join in this time. I had prior commitments.

That next evening, Mother phoned from Washington, D.C.

"Walter Allen, your dad is dead too."

Suddenly, somewhere inside, something felt like concrete. But I listened.

"We found your dad's former boss," Mom continued. "He remembered your dad quite well. But he told us he is dead."

"Of course," continued Mother, "We had to make sure, so we went right to the Office of Vital Statistics. They told us Dad lapsed into a coma several days before he died of cirrhosis of the liver."

Unable to make any words come out of my mouth, I handed the phone to Judy and headed toward the bedroom, tears blurring my vision and burning my cheeks.

I sat on the bed and sobbed. Judy was soon there. An embrace. Assurances.

"Walt, everything will be okay."

How could she know that faithless, dead man was still vital to my security?

The few good memories I had salvaged rushed back. Dad and I together watching the news or an old western, Dad and I together pulling up fresh crabs for supper. Memories such as those had long served as substitutes for approval, love, acceptance. Now a single phone call, and those other memories I had willed into oblivion peered out from behind their poorly disguised hiding places. Dad had quite often failed as a father. He had been downright ruthless at times. His drunken sprees had conditioned me to fear. His grab-the-kids-and-run lifestyle had sparked an insecurity I apparently still was not admitting.

Faithless or not, mean or not, I had loved that man deeply and had wanted him to love me in return. I had wanted his approval, his affirmation. I recalled how, once when I was eleven, I had dreamed that Jesus had returned and my father had not left for heaven. Instead he had continued stumbling drunkenly across the yard with a whiskey bottle in his hand. The dream had seemed so frighteningly real that I had startled myself awake with a over-rapid heartbeat.

Now I could just forget nursing the quiet hope that I would some day make face-to-face contact with the father I had loved at a distance. That was no longer possible. If my need for ongoing security, my wish for lasting significance was ever to be met, I would certainly have to look for it from someone else.

During the next several weeks, I naturally turned over and over some things that might have been and now never could be. But I also began finding it easier and more comfortable to turn my thoughts toward my Heavenly Father. He had never forsaken me. He had always been there for me. He was my Father, and I was his son. This was a different kind of father-son relationship. That was an eternal bond. I could claim His promise, "The Lord is my helper, and I will not fear what man shall do unto me."

Surprisingly, the slow peace that followed that Richter-scale shock of learning about my father's death slowly transferred back to my interactions at the counseling center. I found myself emphasizing God's "Father" relationship with clients hesitant to relax in His love.

Some were anorexic or bulimic young women, starving, binging, or haunting beauty parlors in hopes of overtaking what they thought their husband's attentions could supply—security and significance. Failing, others had become resentful and were seeking to end the very relationships they had so desperately wanted to improve.

One day I told Janet there was several simple statements she needed to share with herself, perhaps even her husband:

"I love you, but I don't need you to assure my mental, emotional, even physical health." "I love you and want to spend the rest of my life with you, but my life will not end if you walk out the door."

"I have found Another Person who is more than able to meet all my needs. Him I call Father."

But if I heard myself asking Janet to own those statements for herself, I felt myself transacting the same thing in my long fantasized relationship with an earthly father. My Heavenly Father became my "Abba" Father, a Companion beyond that of even Creator or Redeemer. For the first time, I could increasingly and personally own the words of the song:

And He walks with me and He talks with me
And He tells me I am His own;
And the joy that we share as we tarry there,
None other has ever known.[1]

Slowly I realized that fear was losing its grip. My Heavenly Father was becoming what my earthly father could never have become. Or rather, should I say, I was allowing my Heavenly Father to be to me what no earthly father could ever be—my life, my strength, my protector. It was freeing not to perform for approval. It was warming not to constantly fear rejection. It was rewarding to begin loving unconditionally. Perhaps greatest of all, it was invigorating to choose to serve—undriven by fear.

---

1 C. Austin Miles, *In the Garden*, Rodeheaver, Co. 1940.

Walter Allen Croom

12 Moving Beyond Fear

It was a good year—1982—not only for the country, but also for Judy and me. While Ronald Reagan, our thirty-ninth president, was presiding over one of the best economic rebounds in recent American history, Judy and I were enjoying the luxury of two cars and a little savings in the bank, and the counseling center was experiencing a steadily ringing phone.

But what brought me even greater satisfaction was the steady spiritual prosperity I was realizing. Over the past four years God had been slowly moving me from a life of fear to a life of faith, and though I had long feared that faith might be as blind as justice, I was—like the hymn writer—increasingly realizing that

Morning by morning new mercies I see:
All I have needed Thy hand hath provided
Great is Thy faithfulness, Lord, unto me![2]

So when I, one March morning, selected from my incoming mail a letter from the General Director of Military Evangelism, Inc., I had no idea that I was about to slit open an invitation to the adventure of my life. Really, the letter contained no invitation of any kind. It was just the familiar, occasional newsletter that Pastor Lilley sent to prayer and financial supporters. It was not what I found in the letter, but

---

2 Thomas O. Chisholm, *Great Is Thy Faithfulness*, Hope Pub. Co., 1951.

rather what I did after reading the letter that brought on an amazing chain of events.

Military Evangelism, Inc. was the parent organization and Pastor Lilley, the resident supervisor of Aberdeen's Servicemen's Christian Center—the place and the person to whom I had turned innumerable times during my spiritually traumatic military stint. Now, the letter said, Pastor Lilley was retiring.

I picked up the phone and dialed. Pastor Lilley answered and, for a minute or two, we made small talk. Then, more out of curiosity than concern, I asked, "Pastor Lilley, who is going to replace you?"

"Well, Walt, when can you come?" Pastor Lilley fired back in his inimitable way. I stumbled through the rest of a suddenly non-committal conversation and put the receiver back on its phone cradle. Such a comment was one I had hardly expected.

Aberdeen. For me, the place—both the military base and the Servicemen's Christian Center—had been virtual proving grounds of both fear and beginning faith. I had left with no intentions of ever returning to do anything. Perhaps visit, but then again leave. Now Pastor Lilley wanted to know if I would do what I had vowed not to do—return to stay.

I don't honestly know if I was flustered or flattered. Such a question was one I didn't really want to answer. At least not at the moment. So I hadn't. But, for some reason, Pastor Lilley wouldn't let that impromptu question go unanswered. He persisted, and a short time later, at his invitation, I did what I was finding myself doing increasingly—stepping beyond my fear.

So it was on the fourth Monday of April that I returned and was interviewed as a possible replacement for Pastor Lilley. And so it was on June 30,

1982, after Judy and I had secured a replacement for the counseling center that I had been privileged to found near Lancaster, PA, that three-year-old Jonathan, five-year-old Joy, thirteen-year-old Paul, Judy, and I headed an overstuffed U-Haul in the direction of Aberdeen.

Was I detouring—again? Or, was I heading back home to where my fear-to-faith venture had begun? I couldn't know...yet.

Really, though, this new ministry afforded no time for the luxury of speculation. The first day I wore the title, I was off to share Psalm 1 with the Lincoln, Delaware congregation of Dr. C. Donald Dibble, the president of the Center's supervisory board. Succeeding days, weeks, months were a repeat. I seemed to always be heading off to some preaching, teaching, or visitation appointment. Or managing a volunteer staff. Or establishing rapport with the constant personnel turnover at the military post we served. Or making contact with current or potential churches. Or thinking of ways to extend the counseling ministry I had enjoyed into a correspondence study program.

Or...But why spend the energy to enumerate? It was just that I simply never ran out of things to do. Exciting as the busyness was, many as the opportunities were, there were problems to solve. For one thing, it became apparent that donor funds were hardly sufficient to adequately support both Aberdeen and its sister Military Evangelism center at Anniston, Alabama. Even maintenance improvements that had been planned at Aberdeen had to be temporarily halted. For example, the center's main roof, which desperately needed to be replaced, would have to await better financial times.

Another faith challenge was the possibility of exclusion from the military post. When I learned from the School Brigade Commander that the Post Chaplain was reluctant to continue accepting our outreach to the military men he pastored and could easily withdraw permission for us to come on post, I immediately set up an appointment and respectfully and personally shared our ministry plans. Of course, I knew some anxiety. My spirit had embraced that kind of fear much too long not to have it invite itself back. It was easy for me to fear that somehow, someway, I might dwindle or even end the kind of personal and spiritual ministry that had been so rescuing, so assuring when I had been a frightened, homesick Aberdeen soldier.

But, between those past and these present Aberdeen days, I had gotten to know the God of all provision and comfort just a little bit more personally, so I willfully turned toward Psalm 127:

> *Except the Lord build the house, they*
> *labor in vain who build it... It is vain for*
> *you to rise up early, to sit up late, to*
> *eat the bread of sorrows. For so he*
> *gives his beloved sleep.*

For the rest of his tenure at the Aberdeen Proving Grounds, I kept that Post Chaplain well informed of the possibilities and plans of our center. God's return on the deliberate faith I put into that faithfulness was to allow me to receive a Citation for Outstanding Service from Col. Marty Walsh as one of the final official acts of his official tenure as Commander of the entire post. Attending the presentation was that same Post Chaplain. I learned that he had been the one to nominate me for the honor.

Other challenges and reassurances came wrapped up in people. I had lived through enough of childhood rejection to learn that people—even those who intentioned otherwise—might sometimes disapprove of what I was or did. I easily identified with the Chaplain's cautions about our outreach, but I do confess that I felt like betrayed King David when a close friend and spiritual brother first withdrew his fellowship and then began an undercover campaign of disapproval and disruption. There were whispered questions. Those I answered in person. There were whispered charges. Those the Board of Military Evangelism investigated and found no truth. There was an unsigned accusatory letter from a person of influence. That proved to be an impersonation. The Board of Military Evangelism reprimanded the offender and affirmed my performance as director.

I especially appreciated the support and mentoring I ongoingly received from Dr. Dibble, president of the Board, probably less because he affirmed my leadership than because I so closely identified with his unaffirmed childhood. He had been conceived out of wedlock and had been placed up for adoption, so I knew he knew what rejection felt like.

But Dr. Dibble had not internalized and externalized the fear I had. Whatever had been his route from then to now, he had become quite the memorable white-shoed, bow-tied, flat-topped gentleman.

Dr. Dibble was widely experienced. As a child he had been privileged to sit on R. A. Torrey's lap. As a youth he had played duets with Homer Rodeheaver, Billy Sunday's famed trumpet player and led music for meetings in which such notables as J. C. Penney had given their testimonies. As an adult, his gospel ministry had taken the form of circuit riding.

Dr. Dibble was jovial. Every occasion prompted a story or a joke. Dr. Dibble was also very wise. He would be my mentor. It would rub off on me. I certainly figured it should because that's what the Biblical proverb had suggested: "He that walks with wise men shall be wise."

The choice was a well-advised one because, for the next several years when the same troubles again percolated to the surface, it prevented me from unthinkingly falling back into my instinctive fear-driven responses. Instead I was freer to recall insights Dr. Dibble had shared with me and Scriptures such as Psalm 75:5-6 or Romans 8:28-29.

One morning, for example, when my secretary found it necessary to warn me some annoyances might resurface, my immediate response was to fear. I felt like going on the offensive, perhaps even retaliating. However, I chose to do what Dr. Dibble had modeled for me—reach out for a promise, "Fear thou not; for I am with you...I will strengthen you...help you...uphold you with the right hand of my righteousness."

It worked. There was more than enough affirmation and strength for me to do what God wanted done. After all, if God was in charge of things, why did I need to be afraid? If trouble was grinding towards glory, why should I waste its energies on worry? Eventually, that dear frustrated partner who had not known he had helped me move toward greater faith, exchanged his earthly address for a heavenly address. Then both of us were free.

But faith served to quell more than personal fears. I was also committed to helping Aberdeen trainees address even more deadly ones. October 23, 1983 served as a typical example. When I answered an early morning ring, it was a young Marine with a simple request, "Could I hop a ride to the Center?"

"Of course. Be right there," I promised.

When a quite shaken young man hopped into my van, he burst out with, "Did you hear about the bombing of the Marine barracks in Beirut?"

Yes, I had. It had been disastrous. A terrorist had just driven a truckload of explosives through the main gates of the military compound in Beirut, Lebanon. He had ended his suicide mission by deliberately ramming the barracks housing both American and French troops. And he had gotten his revenge. Instantly killed with him were 241 American Marines and 58 French soldiers. The young Marine joined us at the Center's worship service that morning, took in the good home-cooked meal our kitchen staff had prepared, then lingered behind when the rest headed back to the post on the return van. I retired to our little on-site apartment for just a bit of rest. In the middle of the afternoon, my son Paul came to find me.

"Dad there's a Marine downstairs to see you," he said.

"What does he want?" I asked.

"He wants to get saved."

Fear had so followed that young man around the Center that afternoon that now he wanted to ask the Lord to help him face it. In truth, he was facing fearful possibilities. The whole Lebanon thing had been escalating since June 1982 when Israel had assaulted Lebanon with full-scale air and sea forces in hopes of removing PLO guerrilla bases. Conflict had erupted between Israel and Syria in the Bekaa Valley, and Israel had bombarded Beirut until Palestinian forces withdrew on August 1. But September had brought the assassination of Lebanon's newly elected president, Bashir Gemayel, and Beirut had been divided into chaotic Christian and Muslim sectors. Now the place was a seething mass of anger and death, and

Marine or not, that young man didn't like the prospects. I was awed to introduce him to the Savior, but I grieved over the heinous and deplorable crime that had brought us together.

That strange combination of death prompting serious thoughts about life was to mark the Center's ministry in an ever-increasing way. The invasion of Granada and Panama repeated the phenomenon. Again, during a six-month buildup, six weeks of air strikes and four days of combat that Saddam Hussein inflicted upon the world, fears of being shipped home in body bags drove young men and women to permit us to help them settle accounts with God.

Occasionally, those who did so were other than American. A Cameroon native, introducing himself as Prince Mynang Peters, first developed a personal friendship with us and then relieved his fear of dying by trusting Christ. Jacob, from Madagascar, not only found the liberation of salvation, but he also found the confidence to return to his Muslim homeland, knowing the potential implications of his profession. Abdullah, a fierce warrior who prayed to Allah five times a day, knew that he might never be able to return to his homeland for both political and physical reasons. However, he turned from that fear to peace in salvation.

Of course, there were those who feared things other than death. Several times, there in our services sat half a dozen Saudi Arabian officers hearing a gospel presentation for the very first time. Attempting that in their native country would have been more than a fear experience. They mostly listened—but they did so very politely.

Then there were those who turned war and its fears to personal advantage. America generously trains ally military personnel. However, there are always those who return to their respective countries and translate their Aberdeen training into fear for their fellow countrymen. Consider Samuel Doe, Master Sgt., one-time president of Liberia. Or General Mohammed Zia of Pakistan. Or Colonel Muammar al Quaddfi of Libya.

What those who pushed the doors of that Center both ways did with their personal fears was both my business and not my business. I felt privileged to share the peace of God with them. I felt pained if they proved uninterested or resistant. This time round at Aberdeen, I was at peace. That first time round, as a soldier, I had been terrorized by Viet Nam. Now here I was, back again, sharing the peace that was calming far more than my own personal fears.

A presentation from Major General Johnnie Wilson for
our work among the foreign
students at Aberdeen Proving Grounds.

A presentation by Colonel Marty Walsh for our work
among the soldiers at Aberdeen Proving Grounds.

13 Too Good To Be True

I no longer considered floor-walking and hand-wringing viable ways of dealing with the fears that frequently piggybacked on problems. But when Lou relocated away from Aberdeen, I did honestly wonder how I could fill the big shoes he had left behind.

For at least half of the three years I had directed the Servicemen's Christian Center, Lou had been my "unofficial" assistant director—preaching, teaching, visiting, shuttling guys back and forth from and to the post, and who knows what else—impromptu. Now I was looking at a short list of volunteers, and even slightly workaholic me couldn't add any more to my schedule.

One very-soon morning, there was a knock at the door.

"Good morning. My name is Fred and I would like to know if you have some work I could do in exchange for food?" said a gentleman I guessed might have been about 55. He stood about 5' 6" tall. He spoke in a baritone voice that had a trained quality about it. His wrinkled and weather-beaten face suggested many hours of outdoor work. He appeared and sounded sincere and genuine enough. I had to at least consider his request even though I knew a center like ours could not become a homeless shelter or an easy hit for advantage-takers. We'd had some of that already. One "overnight" guest had lifted the frozen Easter hams off the counter while our soldier

113

guests had slept. Another fellow had regularly slipped food from our freezer to support his drug habit. But if we ministered only to the loveable, the likeable, the problem-less, we would become more of a social club than an outreach.

I decided to invite Fred in for a meal. We chatted briefly over the meal. Then I walked him to the door.

"Stop by tomorrow morning," I said in parting. "Perhaps I can help you again."

To my surprise, Fred did stop by and I served him up another hearty meal. After several days of knocking on our door each morning, I ended my careful deliberations and took the risk, welcoming Fred to move into the Center on a temporary basis. I couldn't help but wonder what the move did to Fred. He had been living in a tent on the outskirts of town.

Fred moved into the center and immediately became loved and adored by our whole family. An early riser, Fred ate a small breakfast and then spent the day from about 8:30 a.m. until 4:30 p.m. painting, cleaning and doing all sorts of odd jobs. When the children got home from school, they first scampered around the Center hunting for Fred, wondering what he was doing. Then at the end of the day, Fred freshened up and joined our family for the evening meal.

This small, gentle man, about whom we had learned so little, slowly wove his way into the fabric and heart of our family. For some reason, Fred and our oldest son, Paul, became close buddies. Fred even bought Paul two little yellow canaries. We sat them next to the window in the Center dining room, an unfortunate choice, because one day in spring when the windows were open, those little birds escaped their cage and took off out the window. Of course, though once or twice we saw them perched in a tree next to the Center, they loved their freedom and never returned. Perhaps that same urge to flee was what had driven Fred to us. We learned that he had come from a respectable Indiana family. One brother was a farmer, another brother an Army colonel assigned to the Pentagon. Once Fred visited this brother and returned with a distant, far away look in his eyes. I saw that same look surface every time the conversation came uncomfortably close to the subject of his broken marriage. Fred had never really gotten over the pain of spurned love.

During the 1950's, Fred had been in the military. After discharge, he had met and married a young lady, only to come home from work one day to find her in the arms of another man. Shaken by the tragic discovery, Fred had quietly quit his job, dropped out of society, and taken to the road. His home had been the tent on his back, his belongings the few cooking utensils packed inside it. He had wandered from town to town, across thirty-five states, doing odd jobs wherever available. Twice he had vowed to, but never accomplished, walking the whole way across America.

But if Fred's choices had reduced his living conditions to less than ideal, he had certainly not compromised his talents. There were several novels to his credit. It was a pity he had never bothered to publish them. And those fingers. Were they ever gifted. As a child, he had hours on end absorbing the music of Beethoven, Mozart, and Handel. Now when Fred played such classic hymns as *In the Garden*, even tone-deaf persons could almost detect birds chirping in the background. At the Center, people found it hard to believe that Fred had never once taken a music lesson.

As a release, as much as a source of income during his years of wandering, Fred said that he had often played in nightclubs, but that he had eventually given up that weariness. People persisted in offering to buy him liquor, and rather than being forced to constantly refuse something he detested, he had removed himself from nightclubs and nightclub piano playing.

The first July we were convinced that Fred could be trusted alone, we decided to take a family vacation and leave Fred in charge of our quarters. Since he loved camping, I mentioned that he might like to take one of our vehicles and get away for a few days. The suggestion seemed agreeable enough with him.

But when we returned, Fred was not there. Someone at the Center said Fred had left in the van, saying he'd be back before the weekend. But Friday came and went and there was no Fred. Now I knew why Fred had sold the stereo system that we had bought him for his birthday, saying he wanted to buy another tent. He had been planning to move on, and I had not noticed. All that remained of Fred—the man who had walked through our lives and stolen our hearts—were a few clothes we had given him.

That same weekend, we received a phone call from a gas station owner in Western Maryland. Our van had been abandoned at his station. Monday morning Judy and I headed to Western, Maryland and, with a recent picture of Fred handy, drove back and forth, up and down the country roads near the gas station, looking and inquiring. One forest ranger thought he had seen someone that fit Fred's description at a campsite but wasn't absolutely sure. Finally we had to give up our search and head back to Aberdeen.

Fred had been in the habit of calling his eighty-one-year-old mother in Indianapolis almost every week, so I searched for her number among our old telephone records and gave her a call. Just like Fred's, her voice was pleasant. She said Fred had spoken highly of the Center and was surprised to learn that he had left.

"But, that's just like Fred," she added.

Never again during the next twelve months did we hear from Fred. Several times I checked with his mother. She hadn't either. It seemed so unlike Fred not to contact his mother.

Then almost two years to the day of Fred's departure, someone showed up at the Center with information about Fred. I had retired to our Center apartment and was watching the evening news when Paul came to tell me a stranger was downstairs waiting to see me. It was John, a man who had stayed at the Center for a few weeks while Fred had been with us. John had an interesting but strange story I had never heard—about Fred!

While Fred had lived with us, he had felt uncomfortable and visited the doctor. What I had not known was that the doctor had told him that his difficulty was lung cancer, and that he would have about one year to live! Fred had wanted to return to Lake Tahoe, Nevada to die, alone, in a small lean-to he had built with his own hands.

"But why didn't Fred tell me?" I begged.

"Because he was afraid you would insist on taking care of him at the Center."

"Fred made me promise to come back and tell you everything—but not before two years were up," John said with the sadness of one who had kept a painful promise.

Fred still lingers in memory. Oh, I'm sure he was no "angel unawares," but I am convinced that—Just like Dr. Dibble—my relationship with him was the way God met mutual needs in both of our lives. What God did in his life through me, Fred chose not to share. And that's okay. I just know that from my vantage point, Fred came just when I needed extra hands at the Center and left when the volunteer base had again stabilized. It had been so like God to respect both my needs and my fears—sending what I needed when I needed it most.

Dale's habit of out-loud menu planning occasionally announced other opportunities for faith to override fear.

"Walt, we have just enough hamburger meat for the weekend," she explained one day. "Then we..."

A phone rang and I had to hurry away to the office.

"Walt," offered the faceless voice at the other end of the line, "I just called to see if you could use any meat for your freezer." I scampered back to the kitchen.

"Dale, don't worry about that hamburger," I almost laughed. "The Lord has just taken care of it."

It had been our unwritten policy at the mission to not rush out and make purchases without first giving God an opportunity to provide. Of course, we felt it our responsibility to take care of urgent needs such as repairing a furnace on a cold winter night or replacing faulty brake shoes on a vehicle. But we sometimes placed a bucket under a leaking pipe or sidelined a vehicle and let God send someone to meet our need and carry off the blessing of giving.

By now I was beginning to enjoy watching God meet needs and forestalling my fears. It was fun to watch who He tapped on the shoulder to fill in or make up for whatever circumstances prevented me from doing or manipulating into existence. Gene Chandler was certainly one of those who spread God's grace and goodness. Affectionately called

Pastor Chandler, because he had pastored several churches, Gene was another wise and godly man now semi-retired and living in Columbia, South Carolina. Part-time employment trips brought him to Maryland from time to time, and each time he came our way, he showed up at the Center.

I affectionately nicknamed Pastor Chandler "The Lone Ranger" for the simple reason that when one least expected him, he popped in, unnoticeably took care of whatever, and just as quietly vanished. His "Lone Ranger" silver bullet was an ever-ready toolbox or a very timely message—whichever was more appropriate for the moment. No question about it, Pastor Chandler was a whole lot more than a "Lone Ranger." He was a sterling jack-of-all-trades.

On one occasion, Pastor Chandler showed up just after one of our vans went down. He went to the junkyard, retrieved the necessary part and spent all afternoon repairing our much-needed van. On other occasions, he would just stroll through the buildings repairing light fixtures or leaking faucets. There was never a charge. Over the years he must have saved the Center thousands of dollars. There was always that timely word of encouragement. Sometimes I would be so physically worn that I feared collapse, but just like a spiritual genie, Pastor Chandler would show up with a word of encouragement or message from the Lord that renewed both body and soul.

Of course there were others too:

...Ben, a military retiree, who left his imprint on practically every room in the building.

...Carolyn, who frequently filled her car with other cooks and came to spend the day baking up a storm of cookies and cakes. Her cookies became quite the favorite of Post trainees!

...Russ, a civilian deeply interested in our military outreach.

...Brian Britton, a Post grad who married a local girl and became a years-long volunteer.

...Geraldine and Ruth Christy, cooking and cleaning regulars, who were deeply loved by both trainees and their officers.

I had no question Who had brought these people to grace the ministry of the Center. Seeing my Heavenly Father so busily interweaving lives and meshing ministries stirred even greater confidence than my personality could have mustered up had I tried to generate it all by myself.

Yet it was more than people that the Center needed if it was to efficiently serve. President Ronald Reagan, had planked his campaign platform with the promises of both economic revival and military revitalization. So after his election, millions of dollars were sent rushing though the veins of military establishments. A sizable chunk of that money came to Aberdeen for new barracks and other projects.

Many of the soldiers on Post were living in old World War I type barracks—old, drafty, dilapidated barracks that bunked forty soldiers per floor, eighty per building. There was absolutely no privacy, so when new, well-lit, heated, and air-conditioned dormitories that housed no more than four to six per room became the norm, we at the Center knew that we had to upgrade a bit too. Our dorms were situated in the basement. They were damp and musty and, like the old barracks, afforded no privacy.

Hoping to turn the empty area above the gym into a nice modern dormitory, we began a campaign for funds. But some were suspicious of our motivations. One pastor asked me to refrain from discussing our plans for improvement and expansion. I felt the old slide toward discouragement and felt the familiar panic of recurring fear, but thankfully this time, for only a day or two. And even though another gentleman offered the project a local government-funded grant, the Board of Military Evangelism declined the offer. They wanted to keep the work faith-based. I quite agreed. But I was faced with the challenge of support for the work. Part of that challenge was determining a comfortable personal view of money and management. I did not want to fall into the ditch that obviously lay on either side of the financial road.

For a while, I found myself vacillating between the opposite convictions of Bristol's George Mueller and Chicago's D. L. Moody. Without a solitary word of need to anyone, Mueller had prayed into existence an orphanage and onto its often empty tables food for hundreds of orphans. Yet, with just as much faith and boldness, Moody had, with quite the evangelistic fervor he was noted for, buttonholed every potential donor he felt could help him establish and maintain the fledgling Moody Bible Institute he had founded.

At first I agonized over who was right and who was wrong. But I had to eventually conclude that it mattered less whether my monetary convictions earned the approval of others or not. How I cooperated with the Lord's provisions mattered less than that I did. I knew most non-Christians would not accept my message. So did it matter if fellow believers differed on such minor things as fund-raising?

As I sought the mind of the Lord in regard to this matter, I once again turned to the Scriptures. During his travels, the Apostle Paul had made no apology about raising funds for the Jerusalem church. He had never hesitated to share their needs with others, even solicit money. So why should I? On the basis of those personal convictions based on Scripture, we sent out informational letters to our supporters. Back came the necessary money to complete the project. In came volunteer carpenters to tear down, to build up, to complete not only new administrative offices, but also that much needed new dorm complete with twenty bunks graced with new quilts made by volunteer sewing groups, a modern shower, and a nice reading room stocked with several thousand books.

For me, the reward of the venture in faith was seeing the whole thing underwritten by God's people in God's time and in God's way. I hadn't had to help Him worry or fear a bit of it into existence! Maybe that's why the songwriter had said so eloquently:

His love has no limit;
His grace has no measure;
His power has no boundary known unto men.
For out of His infinite riches in Jesus,
He giveth, and giveth, and giveth again.[3]

Yet, if I found my faith increasingly strengthened by the Center's expansion, I also found it equally challenged by a little plot of land and a small mobile home. When Judy and I had returned to Aberdeen in 1982, we had moved back into the same Center apartment that we had lived in during my 1970 and 1971 Aberdeen training days. Then it had been Judy and me and six month old Paul. Now it was thirteen-year-old Paul, five-year-old Joy, and three-year-old Jonathan.

Judy and I would have preferred to raise our children in the country, but though I would have loved to

---

3 Annie Johnson Flint, *He Giveth More Grace*, Lillenas Pub. Co. 1941.

offer them wide open spaces, fresh air, and a good work ethic, I would have to accomplish those goals in some other way. We had chosen the more economical housing of the Center so that we could send our children to a Christian school.

The choice had made Judy and me sacrifice a few of our wishes and may have complicated a few family matters, but our children certainly flourished in many ways. The halls of that little apartment were often filled with excitement and laughter. Joy loved to fill up water balloons, crawl through the two-story window, and drop them on unsuspecting soldiers' heads as they came around the end of the building. Of course, she got what she wanted—water battles to end all water battles. Paul, on the other hand, developed an enviable ministry to the homeless who were naturally attracted to a Center such as ours. And then there was Jonathan, who would think of more mischievous acts than the other two put together. Say, crawling into the bathtub fully dressed...or bringing home stray dogs...or...

Of course, the whole Center was the children's home. From the dorm facility to the chapel and gymnasium, they bounced, jumped, and played, much to the delight of the soldiers. The soldiers were their big brothers and sisters and even when the doors to the Center were officially closed, there were always soldiers frequenting our homes and our lives.

Eventually there came that inevitable day when we knew we must start looking for a home other than our Center apartment. A newspaper ad attracted us to a small property in the northern part of the county. Judy and I rode out to inspect it. It was a large lot improved with a mobile home. It looked good as a present investment to rent out until we could pay it off.

Then we could sell the mobile home and build our dream home.

The day of the auction was exciting. Of course, we could not know whether the many spectators included many serious bidders or not. The place didn't look that inviting since the man who had owned the property had died about a year earlier and his disinterested family had allowed the place to become overgrown and debris cluttered. But we could see the potential, and we were going for that.

To our amazement, we ended up high bidders and therefore buyers. The auctioneer felt that, as had been advertised, the property was a full two acres, but he assured us that there would be a deduction if this proved incorrect. On that word, I wrote a ten-percent down payment check and then called a professional surveyor to confirm or deny the two-acre estimation. When the survey returned just slightly less than the promised two acres, the seller was as good as his word and our purchase price dropped a comfortable four thousand dollars. We were also pleased to learn that the price we had paid for the property was some seventeen thousand dollars below the tax-assessed value.

But, all was not to continue as rosy as it had begun. Though we could put down fifty percent of the asking price, the bank refused our loan request.

"We don't loan money on unimproved land" was their excuse.

Judy and I walked out of the bank. Judy looked at me. "Walt, what are we going to do?"

"We're going to pray about it, that's what," I said a bit more calmly than I felt.

So we did. Repeatedly over the next few days. Back came an inner answer.

Call that pastor friend in Pennsylvania and ask him if he knows of anyone in his church that can help.

Talk about timid. I knew that early rejection had encouraged shyness in me, but now I knew that wouldn't be an excuse the Holy Spirit would appreciate in return for the prompting to contact someone who could help. So I chose to ignore the old pull back to fear and reticence and called. Within a few days, I received a check in the mail for a large sum of money. There was a note attached. It said: no legal work needed. In gratefulness, I had our attorney draft the proper legal document. Within two years, we had returned the entire loan.

There was just no way I could gainsay what the Psalmist had spoken of—*the fear of the Lord is the beginning of wisdom.* It may have taken me years to begin, but if beginnings were to be the stuff of the rest of my life, I would accept them as opportunities for maturing knowledge into experience, experience into faith, and faith into release from lingering fears.

Let the good old Post Office warn all they wanted about "too good to be true." Here the caution just didn't apply.

Judy and I celebrating our 30th
anniversary in London in 1997.

Judy and I taking a day off
from ministry in Trinidad.

Paul

Joy

Our Children

Jonathan

Walter Allen Croom

Appendix I: An Overview

As a small boy, I sometimes followed my mother from room to room—probably what every other little boy occasionally does. But what gave away my unusual attachment to my mother was that as I followed her around, I was firmly gripping her apron strings.

Now, many years later, I can recognize that I was quite a fearful child. The sad thing, of course, is that as I matured in years, I did not lose those fears. Instead, they were made larger and even more threatening by what happened in my home. First, my sister left home—much too young to accept responsibilities. Then, when I childishly took my younger brother's dare but accidentally shot him in the face with a BB gun, my dad gave me an extremely severe lashing. Of course, my brother quickly recovered, but I turned into an emotional wreck. So, it didn't sweeten things for me when Dad decided to get even with Mom by making my brother Donald and me spend Christmas with him away from home. Two years later, after I broke my arm, Dad tried to beat me to teach me not to be irresponsible. Later, it was that horrible ax-swinging incident. And the list could go on.

At the time, the only way I could survive those fears was to develop defense mechanisms. I strictly obeyed my dad's every dictate so I could escape punishment. I daydreamed about success, hoping that reaching some goal might help me reach security and significance. But, of course, my fears only intensified.

In my search for peace, I finally turned to God, but, to my dismay, even that move failed to allay my fear, anxiety, and insecurity. For the next dozen years, I was a near-drowning man, futilely struggling to keep my flagging emotions afloat and functioning. Even in Bible school, I sometimes became so over-whelmed with unnamed anxieties that I was fre-quently plagued with psychosomatic problems.

I know now what I did not know then. God is not man's sedative. Nor is He the entrance to man's ideas of "success." He would function, rather, as the still small voice that I needed to become quiet enough to hear and heed. I needed *Him* more than I needed per-sonal recovery. I had been seeking emotional stabili-ty instead of what He had said to seek—"the Kingdom of God and His righteousness." Thankfully, I slowly discovered that as I sought Him first, then all those things—emotional stability, peace, and freedom from fear and anxiety—became *mine*.

Of course, there still are those days yet when fear revisits me. But when they do, I just snuggle up close to my Heavenly Father and *re*-experience what the prophet of old said—"Thou wilt keep him in perfect peace, whose mind is stayed on thee."

Appendix II: Steps Toward Overcoming Fear

I: Relate to God

Overcoming fear begins by properly relating to God. It is impossible to experience the peace *of* God apart from having peace *with* God. Because God is holy and just, His character demands a penalty for sin. It is absolutely necessary for it to be this way or else His holiness would be less than perfection. A perfect and holy God has standards of perfection. A violation of those standards was what plunged the whole world of mankind into sin and separation from God. According to Scripture, Adam—as the first man—acted for all those who would be in his family. So, when Adam sinned, both he, his family, and all who were yet to be born into his family, were plunged into sin and became guilty before God.

As a holy God demanding perfection, God could no longer walk with sinful Adam or any of his race. Instead, God needed to separate from man and his sin, so he drove Adam from the garden. But God is also a loving and compassionate God. A look at the cross says that much. Man was human and could not atone for his own, so a perfect God satisfied his perfect demands by offering Himself as the perfect sacrifice for sins. In that way God carried out the redemption. He had planned from eternity past—long before man had even sinned. The plan consisted of Jesus, the second person of the Godhead, coming to earth to make atonement for sin. Jesus was ushered into this world by the virgin Mary nearly two thousand years ago in a lowly stable in Bethlehem. A virgin birth was

God's plan to assure that Jesus would be free of the contamination of Joseph's sin-tainted bloodline. Otherwise Jesus could not have been the *perfect* sacrifice for death.

God, in the form of Jesus the Son, stepped down from glory that we might step up to heaven. He died in order that we might live. Outside the city wall on the old rugged cross Jesus died to satisfy the righteousness of God. His death made it possible for mankind to once again be reunited with God the Father.

In order for this transaction to be formalized, each human being needs to receive the Lord Jesus into his or her heart. The Scripture says, "For whosoever shall call upon the name of the Lord shall be saved." By faith, the seeker may bridge this chasm between himself and God. He may, by faith, enter into a right relationship with God the Father.

Simply pray this prayer:

Dear Lord Jesus, I acknowledge to you that I have a wayward nature. I acknowledge that I have violated at least one of the Ten Commandments. I understand that by violating one commandment, I am guilty of violating all of them. I believe that Jesus is the Son of God the second person of the Godhead. I believe that you are God's perfect sacrifice for my sin. I believe that You died that I might live. By faith, I invite You, Lord Jesus, into my heart and life. I am trusting only You to take me to heaven. I look forward to meeting You in heaven. Thank you that you will be with me for the rest of my life. Thank you for your forgiveness and for this wonderful gift of eternal life. Amen.

II. Conquest begins in the mind

A right relationship with God the Father and his Son is the only foundation substantial enough to support you. God is the only person who can bring calmness to your spirit. He is the one person who can help you conquer your fears. The Scripture says, "Perfect love casts out all fear." As you grow in His love, your fears will subside.

Begin facing your fears by looking inward—to your mind. It is your "command center." From there, come your decisions. You use your mind to think, to develop emotions, to order your actions. In short, your mind is the place where you conceive the beliefs of which you operate your life. That is why the Apostle Paul urged you to be renewed in your thinking processes (Ephesians 4:23). In II Corinthians 10:5 he also instructs believers to cast off wrong reasoning. In Philippians 4:8-9 he encourages Christians to exercise right thinking patterns.

Right thinking is important because only *right* thinking can lead to right behavior and healthy emotional responses. Wrong thinking leads to wrong behavior and emotional bondage. It is in your thinking center that you turn the information you have gathered into the core beliefs by which you gauge all your opinions and upon which you make all decisions. Naturally, these beliefs affect your decisions and your emotions.

John Wycliffe spoke of one mother who was tormented that she might not see her deceased child in heaven because the child had not been baptized. Wycliffe was able to lift her spirits by turning her thoughts to the Scripture. Here he pointed out that David's and Bathsheba's infant son had not been baptized before he died. Yet David looked forward to the day when he could go to "be with the child."

Wycliffe also reminded the distraught mother that Jesus had said to the unbaptized thief on the cross beside Him, "This day thou shalt be with me in paradise." The mother took it all in, thought a moment, and then a smile broke across her face. She had changed her core belief and that changed her emotional response.

Some years ago, my wife and I journeyed to the little Caribbean island of Dominica to do counseling workshops and evangelistic preaching. As we approached Dominica, our pilot warned that area wind patterns would create a short period of turbulent conditions, but that we would not need to be concerned because that was usual and they were quite prepared. Sure enough, for several minutes, our small plane shook and trembled. One lady screamed quite loudly, but another—in the seat just ahead of hers—sat quietly while a child on her lap laughed hilariously. It was not the event that produced these two different emotional responses. Rather, it was the interpretation of these events. The vocal lady concluded that her life was in danger and responded by screaming. The child, amused by the unsteadiness of the plane, responded by laughing.

To overcome fear, you need to firm up scripturally sound and emotionally healthy beliefs—the kind that can serve as your shelter in the time of emotional storms. There are at least seven:

God is sovereign *(Psalm 75:6,7)*
God rules *and* overrules. He oversees all nations, His church, and his individual children. It was no accident that Jesus was born at the precise time in history that He was. God had been at work behind the scenes of Nebuchadnezzer's Babylonian Empire, preparing it for Alexander the Great to take over. With

Alexander's kingdom had come Greek—the language the whole known world adopted. So it was that the Apostles could easily share the message of Christ with many nations and ethnic groups. But, at just the right time, God moved the Grecian Empire off the world stage and allowed the Roman Empire with its rule of peace and its Roman roads so that missionaries could easily speed the news that God had "sent forth His Son" (Galatians 4:4).

Clearly, God's sovereign hand put even the nations in the necessary places at the necessary times so that God could become man. These nations did not realize that they were being moved along by the hand of God, that they were helping God to bring about His grand plan for the ages.

In much the same way, God rules and overrules in the life of His Church. Satan has no more power against this invisible body than what God permits. Believers can gain solace from the fact that God is in control. With such a conviction, you need not be controlled by fear.

God is everywhere present *(Psalm 139:7,8)*

No matter where you go in this world, God is there. He sees, He knows, He hears. David reflected this understanding of God's presence in his Old Testament Psalms: "Yea, though I walk through the valley of the shadow of death, I will fear no evil; for thou art with me." In the New Testament, the Lord Jesus said, "I am with you always, even unto the end of the world." David wrote, "I will both lay down in peace and sleep; for you, Lord, only make me dwell safely." So too, you need to accept as your core belief that the Triune God—The Father, Son and Holy Spirit—is always with you. If, like David, you face opposition or even "walk through the valley of the

135

shadow of death," you can face either with the knowledge that God is with you in a very present way. If fear accompanies the experience, God's presence is able to drive it far away.

God is all powerful *(Psalm 9:1)*

No nation, no person can stand against God. Any who challenges God's authority goes down in defeat. Just as a simple computer can never rise up and take over the world, so God's created beings can never usurp authority from the Creator. It is simply unthinkable.

Through God's awesome power, He brought the Israeli people out of Egypt and across the Red Sea. He caused the walls of Jericho to tumble down. With one blow, He eliminated 180,000 of Israel's enemies. The best thing is that this same God is still on the throne and is just as capable of protecting you today as He was in Bible times. The psalmist wrote, "He is the strength of my life; of whom shall I be afraid?" (Psalm 27: 1).

When the children of Israel were about to possess the Promised Land, God told them to be strong and courageous and not to be afraid because He would be with them. It was belief in God's ability to sustain them that kept them going. Fear could not withstand God.

God is your wisdom *(Proverbs 2:6)*

Like most people, you have times when you are unsure about the best course of action. As a result, fear raises its ugly head. God has promised, however, that He will give you wisdom to solve your problems. Since God created the world through the same wisdom He used to intricately design the human mind, you can be sure that it is through your mind and His Word that He will share His wisdom with you. That is why you do not need to fear.

God is your helper *(Hebrews 13:6)*

Helping is not a foreign concept. You do it all the time and in many different ways. You help your children; you assist a needy neighbor. In the same way, God is your helper. He helps because he loves. So it is your privilege to claim the promise, "I will not fear what man shall do unto me."

God is faithful *(Deuteronomy 7:9)*

When people get married, they exchange vows and make promises—to love, cherish, and remain together until death. Yet, many break those promises. But God is faithful to all His promises. He never leaves nor forsakes. He honors all His commitments. He keeps all His promises.

You are special to God

God loves you and cares for you as much as you care for your children. His great sacrifice for salvation is proof of that. Only a compassionate and loving God who cares deeply about you would have done such a thing. It is true that apart from the Lord Jesus, you are and have nothing. But in Christ, you are:

...**chosen** (John 15:16)

...**seated in the heavenlies** (Ephesians 2:6)

...**a child of God** (John 1:12)

...**part of a royal priesthood** (I Peter 2:9)

...**a joint heir with Christ** (Romans 8:17)

Truths such as these can transform your fear and anxiety into confidence and assertiveness. Fear enslaves, but truth liberates. Jesus said, "You shall know the truth and the truth shall make you free" (John 8:32). As you develop core beliefs about God and your relationship with Him, your spirit is freed to love, honor, and serve the One who created you and died to redeem you.

Overcoming fear is the result of walking by faith. Faith is believing that God blesses as you obey Him (Hebrews 11:1,6). One hymn writer put it simply: "Trust and obey for there's no other way to be happy in Jesus but to trust and obey."

It is in the obedience of faith that you may encounter your greatest challenge. You may desire to believe God and to submit to His Fatherly guidance, but there may come those times when you feel as threatened as a novice being asked to climb in the wheelbarrow a tightrope walker plans to wheel across the Niagara Falls. You may *know* that your Heavenly Father is able to get you across your life-sized "Niagara Falls," but you may not *feel* like climbing into the wheelbarrow of circumstances He is using to do it.

Take, for example, the challenges a believer feels when he decides to challenge his life-long bouts with claustrophobia. He wants to overcome it, but to do so, he should do more than merely challenge the fear. He should first develop strong core beliefs about the person of God and his own personal relationship with Him. Then he might memorize verses of Scripture about God's character, perhaps reduce those most helpful to easy-to-remember reminders like:

God is in control
God is present with me
God is all powerful
God is faithful
God is my protector
God is my strength
God is my helper

With such helpful self-reminders, you can then begin your faith-walk. Perhaps it will prove something like what our daughter Joy experienced on her first trip to the beach. I saw that she was terrified by that much water, so I put her little hand in mine and walked with her along the shoreline. As we walked, I talked to her about God and His beautiful creation. Little by little, I nudged her towards the water. She flinched when it first hit her toes, but I did not pull her away. Eventually, the water crept up to her ankles, then her knees. Finally, she transferred her anxiety to me as her parent and allowed the fear to run its own dying course.

Of course, not all fears are that small and can be dealt with that simply. Yet, if you recognize a fear that you must deal with in faith, you need to take those first small steps toward obedience. Five steps up a ladder may be a humble beginning toward overcoming a fear of heights, but it is a start. Unchallenged fear usually takes over; it turns into a formidable foe.

As a young adult, I sometimes fearfully pulled the shades and locked the doors of our little house. In time, I could not go to bed without also locking and placing a chair against my bedroom door. I became a prisoner in my own home. To rid myself of this fear, I first developed some strong core beliefs about the personhood of God and my relationship with Him. Then I put my faith into practice and left my bedroom door unlocked. I knew I had moved away from fear to faith when I recently realized that I sometimes forget to lock any of our house doors at night!

As you begin taking such small steps toward faith, your faith will increase. Eventually, you will be able to obey as much as Abraham obeyed when God asked him to leave his homeland with out the sure promise of where he was going. Abraham simply acted on God's request and began his journey. But on the way, when a food shortage occurred, Abraham tried solving the problem himself by going down to Egypt.

Then, when he realized that the loveliness of his wife might occasion a problem, he asked Sarah to tell people that she was his sister. That was not true. Abraham's faith also failed when he couldn't wait for God to fulfill his promise of a son. After what seemed too long a delay, Abraham gave into the suggestion of his wife Sarah and took the slave girl Hagar as his secondary wife and produced a son that occasioned much strife.

Nevertheless, God kept His promises, and in time Sarah also gave birth to a son. When God tested Abraham by asking him to sacrifice his son, Abraham chose to obey God completely. He rose up early in the morning and started to the place of sacrifice. But you know how the story ended. God provided a ram so that Abraham could offer it in the place of his son. The reason Abraham was finally able to submit in faith and to obey was that he had, in the meantime, grown accustomed to a daily walk with God. He had come to trust full in God's integrity. In much the same way, as you walk by faith, humbly submitting to His voice, your faith will increase and your fears will subside. Like Abraham, you may wobble for a while, but in time you will come to realize that God is a trustworthy partner.

There are several steps you can take to increase your faith:

Keep a prayer journal
As God answers your prayers, go back and note the answer. Review your prayer journal often, It will prove to be a source of encouragement and strength.

Do a character study
Check out what God has to say about the "heroes of faith" he has listed in Hebrews 11. Witness *how* they put their faith in God.

Read biographies of godly persons

Like Enoch, many have walked with God. Read their struggles, their victories.

Rejoice in the Lord

God told numerous prophets about the judgment Israel deserved and would receive. One of them, Habakkuk, trembled in fear at the thought of its severity. Yet, rather than letting the news of Judgment get him down, Habakkuk chose to turn his thinking toward His Heavenly Father and to rejoice in the God of his salvation:

> When I heard, my belly trembled, my lips quivered at the voice; rottenness entered into my bones, and I trembled in myself, that I might rest in the day of trouble...Although the fig tree shall not blossom, neither shall fruit be cut off from the fold, and there shall be no herd in the stalls; Yet I rejoice in the Lord, I will joy in the God of my salvation (Habakkuk 3:16-18)

Practice the faith-walk

Exercising faith is like exercising muscles. The more you exercise them, the stronger they become. In the same way, exercised faith leads to confidence and boldness. Faith is an effective deterrent to fear and anxiety. Fear cannot control as long as we firmly adhere to our core beliefs about God and our relationship to Him. Fear cannot conquer as we practice faith-walking.

Appendix III:

Practical Exercise

1. Write down several causes for fear.
   I John 4:18,19_____
   Proverbs 28:1 _____
   Proverbs 1:33 _____
   Genesis 32:11 _____

2. Write down several results of fear.
   Luke 21:16 _____
   Genesis 3:10 _____
   Jonah 1:3 _____
   Genesis 12:12-13 _____
   Matthew 26:69-75 _____

3. According to Ephesians 4:23 the battle to conquer fear must be waged where?

   _____

4. According to II Corinthians 10:5 the believer is to discard

   _____

5. According to Philippians 4:8 the believer is to think right

   _____

6. According to the following verses, why should we not fear?
   Psalms 23:4 _____
   Isaiah 41:10 _____
   Isaiah 43:2 _____
   Psalms 37:3 _____
   Jeremiah 33:3 _____
   Philippians 4:19 _____

Psalms 27:1 _____

Psalms 4:8 _____

Daniel 4:17 _____

Psalms 75:6,7 _____

Romans 8:37-39 _____

Hebrews 13:6 _____

7. What blessings come to the believer as a result of trusting God?

Proverbs 28:1 _____

Isaiah 26:3 _____

Proverbs 14:26 _____

Psalms 34:4 _____

Joshua 1:9 _____

Proverbs 3:5,6 _____

Psalms 37:3-5 _____

Proverbs 9:10 _____

Proverbs 19:23 _____

Bibliography

Chisholm, Thomas O. *Great Is Thy Faithfulness*, Hope Publishing Co. 1951.

Johnson-Flint, Annie *He Giveth More Grace*, Lillenas Publishing Co. 1941.

Miles, C. Austin, *In the Garden*, Rodeheaver, Co. 1940.

Institute of Christian Counseling

Walt Croom, Ph.D.
Founder-Director

A Lay Course of Study by Extension
Certificate Offered at the Conclusion of Course

About the Course

The Institute of Christian counseling is a professional course of study that is designed to give a thorough working knowledge of the fundamental principles of Christian Counseling.

There are three phases to this course of study, each building upon the other. The first phase lays the foundation while the second deals with specific areas of concern. The third phase gives the student the opportunity to employ what he has learned from the first two phases by working his way through the Counselor's Casebook.

Phase I

Eight Cassette Tapes:

1A Basic Presuppositions

1B Basic Presuppositions

2A Mental Illness?

2B General Principles

3A Directive Counseling

3B Effecting Biblical Change

4A Effecting Biblical Change

4B Effecting Biblical Change

5A Data Gathering

5B Helping through Homework

6A Helping through Homework

6B Reconciliation Principles

7A Depression

7B Depression

8A Depression

8B Depression

Phase II

Six Cassette Tapes:

1A Why Marriages Fail

1B Role of the Husband

2A Role of the Wife

2B Communication

3A Effective Teaching

3B Teenage Rebellion

4A Finances

4B Jealousy

5A Pressure

5B Bitterness

6A Self Image

6B Demon Possession

Endorsements

"Institute of Christian Counseling"

"I am enjoying the course very much. It is obvious that you have spent many hours of research and study to come up with such an exhaustive and complete course. You have truly done mankind a great service."

Hamburg, Iowa

"I am being so blessed by these studies, it has been one of the richest studies I have ever undertaken, may God richly bless you for your work."

Foss, Oklahoma

"I have learned more about Christian Counseling from this course than I ever learned in all my seminary training on counseling theories and methods."

Columbus City, Indiana

"This course has been so fantastic that it has demanded all my extra attention since I received the tapes, etc. Thank you for offering it and please feel free to use me as a reference to other ministers."

Belton, Texas

"I want you to know that I have enjoyed immensely the series of lessons and tapes and will always treasure them."

Carsonsville, Michigan

"I felt I just must write and tell you how I am being blessed by your Christian Counseling material. I would highly recommend this material to every Christian as it would be of such help in every walk of life."

Statesville, North Carolina

"I wanted you to know that thus far I have enjoyed the course immensely and have found it a challenge, and a blessing to me in every way. It is a challenge to delve into new areas and then to re-study things long forgotten. I would urge folks to sign up for the course and that without reservation."

Augusta, Georgia

"I would like to take a few minutes to tell you that the Institute of Christian Counseling course is helping me to meet very specific needs in the lives of the many people I contact in my Christian walk. As Galatians 6:1 tells us, we are to restore a Christian who is overtaken by a fault in the spirit of meekness. I believe your I.C.C. course has equipped me for this commandment."

Texas City, Texas

Beginning
A
Counseling
Center

Walt Croom
with Elaine Huber

Table of Contents

REVIEWS

"I have listened to the taped instructions as well as having read the Manual on Beginning a counseling Center. I have found them to be very informative Any person desiring to establish a counseling center would profit by having this information."

Dothan, Alabama

"Walt Croom's book Beginning a Counseling Center certainly contains all that one needs to 'get started'. There is something for everyone who wants to get involved in counseling. The part of the book that was most useful for me was the section on promotion. There are some ideas that are given that will work, If you will work I highly recommend this book."

Hood River, Oregon

"I have appreciated both the tape and the book. After reading the book and listening to the tape I have taken steps to put several principles into practice. I am working with an attorney on incorporation He now is reading through the manual. We are planning to use the concepts given to plan and prepare necessary documents. Your detailed information with examples have been helpful. In developing our Christian Counseling Service it has been important to find those who are doing it and be able to have their input available. Thank you for your help through this material."

Christian Counseling
Northumberland, Pennsylvania

Walter Allen Croom

Christian Counseling Publications   **$3.95**

- GET THE MOST OUT OF LIFE
- CONTROL YOUR FEELINGS
- CONQUER GUILT
- FIND PEACE OF MIND

WALT CROOM

Table of Contents

What Christian Leaders Say:

"Here you will find practical, straight-from-the shoulder help for depressed people coupled with loving, sensitive concern. Its biblical base is skillfully woven into the material lending the note of God's authority to all counseling and helping the reader weigh all the material in light of the Scriptures."

John Battler, D.Min.
Director Christian Counseling & Education Foundation

"Winning Over Depression has been a tremendous source of information for classroom use. My teaching and counseling are richer because of this book."

Thomas R. Rodgers, D.Min.
President Vice President
Trinity Theological Seminary

"Winning Over Depression presents a candid, Biblical, and practical approach to a very common problem. This Balanced approach will not only help you, but help you to help others."

Gilbert A. Peterson, Ed.D.
President
Lancaster Bible College

Walter Allen Croom

Overcoming Fear
Order Form

Ship To: (Please Print)

Name _____

Address _____

City, State, Zip _____

Day Phone _____

	Price	Quantity	Total
Overcoming Fear	$7.95 ea	_____	_____
Winning Over Depression	$3.95 ea	_____	_____
Beginning a Counseling Center	$14.95 ea	_____	_____
Institute of Christian Counseling (Home Study Training Program)	$225.00 ea	_____	_____

Postage and Handling $1.50 per book _____

(MD Residents add 5% tax) _____

Total Amount Enclosed: _____

Make Checks Payable to:

Christian Counseling Publications
PO Box 878
Aberdeen, MD 21001